BODY AT THE MELBOURNE CLUB

David Burke OAM, a former journalist with the Melbourne *Herald* and *Sun* and the *Sydney Morning Herald*, has made six visits to Antarctica and written three books on the subject: *Monday At McMurdo*; *Moments Of Terror: The Story Of Antarctic Aviation*; and *Voyage To The End Of The World: With Tales From The Great Ice Barrier*. He and Dr P. G. Law are the first (and so far, only) Australians to make a direct flight from Australia to the South Pole when they were members of a long-range US Navy crossing of the bottom of the world. David lives in the Southern Highlands of New South Wales. This is his 22nd book.

By the same author

Novels

Monday at McMurdo

Come Midnight Monday (also produced as a seven-episode ABC TV drama)

Darknight

Non-fiction

Railways of Australia

Great Steam Trains of Australia

Changing Trains

The Observer's Book of Steam Locomotives

Man of Steam

Kings of the Iron Horse

With Iron Rails

Road Through the Wilderness

The World of Betsey Throsby

Making the Railways

Moments of Terror: The Story of Antarctic Aviation

Juggernaut: Sydney's Wild Steam Tram Days

Dreaming of the Resurrection: A Reconciliation Story

Australia's Last Giants of Steam

Voyage to the End of the World: With Tales from the Great Ice Barrier

American Steam on Australian Rails

Roaring Through the 20s

Life of Mary Ward (video)

Great Scott! (musical)

Julian: A Man Condemned? (dramatisation)

BODY AT THE MELBOURNE CLUB

Bertram Armytage, Antarctica's Forgotten Man

DAVID BURKE

Wakefield Press

Wakefield Press
1 The Parade West
Kent Town
South Australia 5067
www.wakefieldpress.com.au

First published 2009
Copyright © David Burke, 2009

Cover designed by Liz Nicholson, designBITE
Text designed and typeset by Clinton Ellicott, Wakefield Press
Printed and bound by Hyde Park Press, Adelaide

National Library of Australia Cataloguing-in-Publication entry

Author: Burke, David, 1927–   .
Title: Body at the Melbourne Club: Bertram Armytage,
               Antarctica's forgotten man/David Burke.
ISBN: 978 1 86254 833 6 (pbk.).
Notes: Includes index.
               Bibliography.
Subjects: Armytage, Bertram.
               Explorers – Antarctica – Biography.
               Explorers – Australia – Biography
               Antarctica – Discovery and exploration.
Dewey Number: 919.8904

Government
of South Australia

Arts SA

fox creek
wines

To Catherine and the three Js.
Together, we discovered Bertram.

CONTENTS

FOREWORD

BY HER EXCELLENCY,
PROFESSOR MARIE BASHIR AC CVO

Body at the Melbourne Club is a moving account of an Australian who deserves to be remembered as an intelligent, sensitive man, and a significant member of the British Antarctic Expedition of Ernest Shackleton in 1907–1909.

One cannot but be deeply moved by many aspects of the character and strivings of Bertram Armytage, whose life came to a dramatic and tragic end in the Melbourne Club. One might justifiably assert that his death occurred at a time when he deserved to be enjoying the acclaim and appreciation of colleagues and of the wider society.

Clearly, Bertram suffered a major depression at the time of his death, a condition that had perhaps affected him intermittently through earlier years. He was continually striving to achieve and in this endeavour, he was also 'action oriented'. His place amongst his siblings as the youngest of four brothers, none of whom were failures, may have been a motivating force in his efforts to realise a life of worth and fulfilment. His father too, was a successful man. Indeed the family name was synonymous with the pioneering efforts and prosperity of colonial Victoria.

An environment of male company consistently reflects the pattern of his life: at school, on the family rural properties, at the University of Cambridge, serving in the Boer War, seriously committed to sporting prowess, and finally, as a member of the Antarctic expedition. Even the choice of his last hours and death – a death executed in a meticulous, militaristic fashion – takes place in the gentlemen's domain of the Melbourne Club.

The reader will be quietly impressed time and time again, by many aspects of his character through comments made by colleagues in Antarctica and also by the Menzies Hotel and Melbourne Club staff. To his comrades in the expedition, he was dependable and loyal – qualities ascribed on several occasions. In summary, he was 'one of the best'.

Significantly however, Bertram suffered a serious setback in the Antarctic, as the story relates, including a loss of self-worth through this unexpected event. And as winter darkness descended, he began to perceive himself as something of a misfit. Nevertheless, he went on to accept confidence-building roles from Shackleton, his leader, in being sent 'into the unknown' and undertaking the leadership of an exploring party.

Inevitably, the great Antarctic adventure came to an end, and though honoured and decorated in London, Bertram is confronted with an sense of inadequacy and alienation, perhaps initiated through his rejection for service in the post for which he felt qualified.

His plea for help at this time of psychological need is directed unsuccessfully to two of his male companions. In despair, does he perceive no relevance to his life?

It is not uncommon to encounter men like Bertram, reserved by nature, idealistic and committed, who consider that they have failed to reach their potential, and by extension, feel an overwhelming sense of worthlessness and beyond hope.

An incomplete component in the mosaic of Bertram's life is his relationship with Blanch, his wife. It would be unfair to place blame for an apparently unfulfilled marriage on either party. Bertram's commitments resulted in absences on service in the Boer War, on shooting expeditions, and finally through his involvement in the exploration of Antarctica. Perhaps Blanch was unable to respond to the needs of a man who found it difficult to ask for acceptance and love, yet quietly craved it.

On his return to London with Shackleton at the triumphal conclusion of the expedition, his wife is living in Surrey with their little daughter. Does she not want to be at his side; does he not have a desire to join them at the village? Instead, he goes home to Australia, and the mystery of his death soon follows.

Did he leave behind a lonely woman, one still young, who had herself felt abandoned? For on receiving the news of Bertram's death, Blanch responds that she could not return to Australia 'for seven months'.

Indeed, there is much to reflect upon in this thoughtful, carefully researched and empathic story, whose publication will coincide with the centenary of Australia's burgeoning interest in and exploration of Antarctica.

Professor Marie R. Bashir AC CVO
Governor of New South Wales

PREFACE

Sir Ernest Shackleton made three voyages of discovery to Antarctica and died on the fourth, at South Georgia (1922) aged 48, before his ship reached the Antarctic Circle.

From the first expedition (1902) he was invalided home after sledging with Scott, the leader, and Wilson – two tragic victims of polar conquest – 380 miles into an unknown continent. His third expedition (1915), when *Endurance* was locked and lost in the Weddell Sea pack, has become the stuff of books, television drama and movies to the present day. He led all his team of 27 men to safety but his plan to march across Antarctica was dashed and in this sense it failed as a venture of discovery.

It is Shackleton's return to the South with his British Antarctic Expedition of 1907–1909 which unfolds as one of the great epics of the polar heroic age. It was the BAE, conceived and inspired by a remarkable leader of men, that Bertram Armytage had the good fortune to join, and participate in the feats of climbing Mount Erebus, the attainment of the South Magnetic Pole, Shackleton's 'near miss' in reaching the Geographic South Pole, leadership of the Western Party, plus assisting in an ambitious research program. This story is not intended as a definitive account of the BAE. Rather, and as far as records allow, it is seeing the expedition as Bertram, the first Australian-born man to go to

Antarctica, would have lived through it from the hut at Cape Royds.

The Armytage quest reaches out to 1944 when Betram's grand nephew, Rex Armytage, saved his life of 11 years by jumping into a dam when a disastrous bushfire consumed his family home, Strathvean, at Cressy in western Victoria. The same fire that reduced the Armytage property to ashes and killed 9000 sheep also burnt, Rex believes, the only existing records of Bertram Armytage, the first Australian-born member of an Antarctic expedition: 'a man who knew no fear.'

Bertram is left to us a figure devoid of footsteps across history's pages. Of a life led amid the squattocracy of western Victoria and the elite of Melbourne society, on a privileged path into Geelong Grammar School, University of Cambridge, big game hunting and the cavalry of the South African War and finally Antarctica, we have neither diary, letters nor notes; just a solitary newspaper interview.

But any man who pits his fragile canoe against The Rip of Port Phillip Bay, who helps row Jesus College to victory, whose marriage makes high society news, who joins the Dragoon Guards to fight the Boers, who is enlisted by Shackleton to lead the Western Party up the Ferrar Glacier, is decorated in London by royalty, and who finally comes home to shoot himself at the Melbourne Club, has to be worthy of a story. This, then, is a reconstruction of the strange, adventurous and troubled life of Bertram Armytage, Antarctica's forgotten man.

David Burke

Armytage v. Armitage

Bertram Armytage is not to be confused with Lieutenant Albert Armitage who was Captain Scott's second-in-command of the British National Antarctic Expedition, 1901–1904. Cape Armitage is a feature of Ross Island in McMurdo Sound.

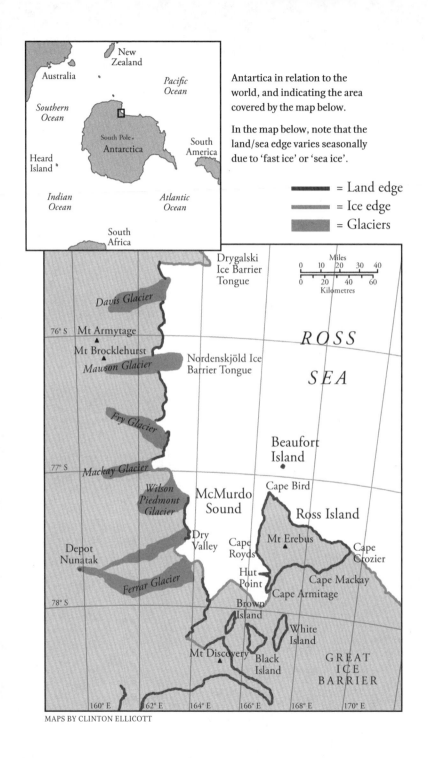

New
Zealand

Australia

Pacific
Ocean

Southern
Ocean

South Pole
Antarctica

South
America

Heard
Island

Indian
Ocean

Atlantic
Ocean

South
Africa

Antartica in relation to the
world, and indicating the area
covered by the map below.

In the map below, note that the
land/sea edge varies seasonally
due to 'fast ice' or 'sea ice'.

= Land edge
= Ice edge
= Glaciers

Drygalski
Ice Barrier
Tongue

Davis Glacier

76° S   Mt Armytage

Mt Brocklehurst

Mawson Glacier

Nordenskjöld Ice
Barrier Tongue

Fry Glacier

77° S   Mackay Glacier

Wilson
Piedmont
Glacier

Depot
Nunatak

Ferrar Glacier

78° S

160° E

162° E

164° E

166° E

168° E

170° E

Miles
0   10   20   30   40
0   20   40   60
Kilometres

ROSS

SEA

Beaufort
Island

Cape Bird

McMurdo
Sound

Ross Island

Dry
Valley

Cape
Royds

Mt Erebus

Cape
Crozier

Hut
Point

Cape Mackay

Cape Armitage

Brown
Island

White
Island

Mt Discovery

Black
Island

GREAT
ICE
BARRIER

MAPS BY CLINTON ELLICOTT

CHAPTER 1

THE WESTERN PARTY

Of all the mountains I've known in Antarctica, none seems more sad and alone than the white-domed peak at 76°02'S. and 160°45'E. on the blizzardly fringe of Victoria Land where Mount Armytage rises 1855 metres above the snow. Countless mountains, and many of more dramatic profile and dizzier in height, thrust through the polar icecap, but Mount Armytage is the one that haunts my memory. In lonesome isolation it personifies the strange and complex life of its namesake, the first Australian-born Antarctic explorer.

The mid-winter wind that whistles down Collins Street in Melbourne is surely sired in McMurdo Sound. Overcoat-clad, I pause on the footpath at the top end of this prestigious city thoroughfare, 'the Paris end' as the publicists call it, gazing up at a window of a squat, grey-faced building across the street. It is the Melbourne Club, venerable, dignified, ever-so-male respectable, and needing quite a pedigree to join when Armytage father and sons were about.

One of the upstairs windows facing into Collins Street will be room 24; or would have been number 24 on the evening of Saturday, 12 March 1910 when Bertram pinned the polar medals to his breast, lay comfortably on the floor and put a gun to his head.

Across 40 years of Antarctic travel, I have many times crossed paths with Bertram Armytage; down the shores of McMurdo

Sound, over by Back Door Bay where stands his little Cape Royds hut, out on the immensity of the Great Ice Barrier where this first Australian marched beside a Shackleton intent on conquering the Pole; and along the coast beneath the glistening, chaotic face of the Ferrar Glacier where he led the Western Party, and all of them lucky to escape with their lives.

The challenge is in following him to the end. Reconstructing the life of an elusive and frustrating character who left no personal record is not a simple task. The nosing and probing skills of old newspaper days are called into play, as are the friends in numerous strategic places who are willing to join in the dig.

For an introduction, we skid across those years to Melbourne morning newspapers of Monday, 14 March and the bold head-lines – Notable Career Ended . . . Suicide of Mr Bertram Armytage.

Constable Bourke's report, as related in the *Age* and the *Argus*, with some irritating contradictions, tells us that Bertram came in a cab from Menzies Hotel, which he frequented, and had his port-manteau taken upstairs to room 24. This was late on the Saturday afternoon, and he was observed to be wearing the sort of going-out suit that is normal for a squattocracy fellow with expensive tastes. His choice of the Melbourne Club is interesting; why he would decide to do something tragic and messy at this most respected address where the Armytage name had been prominent for decades, can only be linked to a mind deeply depressed. Uncle Charles Henry, the man who had owned magnificent Como estate across the river, was a distinguished member and Uncle Ferdinand Felix was another, not to speak of his own father, Frederick of Wooloomanata. Bertram's brother Harry's gift of the gold Williamstown Racing Club cup shone in a cabinet, while a relative of his mother's side, Harold Werribee Staughton, was a former Club president. It was indeed Armytage territory in which he decided to die.

According to the *Age*, a few Club members on hearing a shot ran upstairs and found the door jammed (as it turned out to be) by a chair propped against it from inside. When they managed to enter,

Bertram Armytage lay on a carefully spread counterpane, pillows beneath his head, polar medals at the breast of his dinner suit, and a smile on his face. The bullet had entered cleanly through the left temple in a single shot. A colt revolver lay by his side.

Members and their guests who sat down to dinner in the front dining room also heard the gunshot but believed it to be noise from the traffic going by among the cable trams in Collins Street. 'Oh, another tyre has burst,' said one of them in the *Age*. (And full marks to the *Age* reporter who managed to get someone who had been to the Melbourne Club to say anything at all.)

Both papers made a brief reference to Blanch (otherwise known as 'Bon') Armytage who appeared to live apart from her husband after he had done with his duty of partaking in Shackleton's victorious return to London with his British Antarctic Expedition. Perhaps Blanch preferred gentlemen more socially acceptable than Bertram's comrades-in-ice. Sir Philip Brocklehurst would have suited but Bertram found his company too uncomfortable after they shared a cubicle in the hut at McMurdo Sound and a three-man sleeping bag on the Ferrar Glacier. According to a young Raymond Priestly (a future vice-chancellor of the University of Melbourne) it wasn't much fun having two men who were at loggerheads in a small tent with you amid the frozen wilds of Antarctica. More of Priestly's words are worthy of analysis as he speaks of how the suicide might have been prevented. 'We returned to Sydney just in time to miss an S.O.S. from Bertram Armytage, who was obviously in mental distress. Had we been home when his message arrived we could doubtless have given him hope.'

Mystery surrounds his suicide. What was this mental distress? Others have asked, on reading the press reports, how was it that Blanch let her husband sail home to Melbourne, alone, when Antarctica had parted them for something like two years? A good question. There was a hint of an affair in London with another member of the Victorian squattocracy which is the sort of talk to set an old journo's nostrils twitching.

COMO

People on the National Trust circuit know Como as the elegant Italianate double-storeyed mansion close by the river at South Yarra. Bertram spent quite a lot of his young life at the family's big white city house that his uncle, Charles, bought for £14,000 in 1864, five years before Bertram was born. Charles enlarged it with billiards room and ballroom and lavishly entertained to match. Once Como encompassed 54 acres reaching down to the Yarra, with citrus orchards and cattle grazing among tall grass, the sort of place where a young man could expend his energies in huntin', shootin', and fishin'. Bertram was aged seven when Uncle Charles died, leaving his widow, Caroline, with nine children and the responsibility of managing their vast properties, Fulham and Mount Sturgeon, which she did most capably.

But after her early married years spent in the isolation of Fulham Station, 50 miles from the nearest doctor, Caroline decided it was time to take her young family, plus governess, maids and two milking cows, on a grand world tour that lasted four years. In Caroline's absence, Bertram's father leased the property as a city residence for he and his wife and their four sons; this was when Bertram came to know Como, a place of lavish balls and fancy-dress parties, and where Nellie Melba sang.

At Como the proud antlers of the red deer that Bertram shot await you in the hallway. I am taken to the upstairs nursery and shown a portrait in oils of a golden-headed infant wearing what seems to be a blue-ribboned dress. But it is a boy. It is Bertram Armytage, and Liz, my guide and National Trust curator, believes he was about 12 months old, when all little boys wore dresses. From a store next to the landing, Liz retrieves the portrait of a serious-looking young man. This is Bertram, aged about 22, when he would be paused between coming back from Cambridge and going to war.

Liz leads the way downstairs to the grand billiards room and points to the wall. High above are the Armytage oars from Jesus

College and, more important to my quest, beneath them a neat glass cabinet adorned with the Armytage coat of arms, *Semper Paratus* (always ready). Hanging inside are the Queen's Medal with three clasps from the South African campaign, next to it the King's Medal with two clasps (Queen Victoria had died in the meantime); next to them, the silver Polar Medal for the British Antarctic Expedition 1907–1909, awarded at Buckingham Palace by King Edward VII, and a medallion from the King of the Belgians. Four small metal disks that encompass much that was meaningful in Bertram's life.

Behind a high red-brick wall at Kew, the burial took place two days after the coroner granted permission for the release of the body which had been taken hurriedly from the Melbourne Club to A. A. Sleight's city funeral chapel. The coffin was carried from Como's front door and through ornate iron gates that had been witness to Bertram's many comings and goings. In fact, one story that is still persistent though discredited, suggests Como is where he shot himself, and his body was taken secretly to the Melbourne Club; hard to believe.

George Chirnside, of Werribee Park, was the chief pallbearer, others were his Staughton cousins and Rob Cornish, manager of the Melbourne Club who had Bertram's last note (never made public), and Alex Dyce Murphy, the racehorse owner whose cross-dressing son, a supposed British military spy, wanted to join Shackleton but had been turned down for a reason not too difficult to detect, which led to Bertram Armytage finding a place in the British Antarctic Expedition.

CHAPTER 2

ARMYTAGE COUNTRY

A 20-minute drive into the countryside north from Geelong took me to Elcho where Bertram was born on 29 September 1869, the fourth son of Frederick William and Mary Susan Armytage. The formidable bluestone residence, referred to as 'one of the most unusual and picturesque Gothic revival style homesteads in Victoria' stands beyond a cluster of sugar gums, aloof from passing traffic on the Bacchus Marsh road. With high roof and a set of dormer windows, and framed against a rising hillside, it occupies a once stopping place for Cobb & Co. coaches carrying newcomers from Corio Bay to the Ballarat diggings.

Peter, my obliging guide and a Geelong historian, said Elcho had known a variety of residents since John Galletly, a Geelong bank manager married to Elizabeth Armytage, built it on a lease of 7000 acres in 1867. Prue Acton, the noted fashion designer, and her husband, Mike Treolar, were more recent owners. Soon after Bertram's arrival, his parents moved the family to Woloomanata, a grand house at nearby Lara, which Frederick had built from basalt quarried on the site. Much of Bertram's troubled history would be recorded at Wooloomanata.

In the second half of the 19th century, Australia's wealth flowed from the sheep's back. By 1860, some six million sheep were grazing on the pastures of Victoria. Australian wool was found to be finer, stronger, lighter and cheaper than the old wools of Europe and America, and the appetite of the British mills proved insatiable. Sparked by the gold rush, the colony's population rose sevenfold between 1851 and 1860 – from 76,000 to 540,000 people. These numbers contained the seeds of industry, employment – and opportunity. For those early pioneers who had secured themselves on the land with a mob of sheep, there need be no looking back; the opportunity lay open for the making of a wealthy class of pastoralist, known otherwise as the squattocracy.

Bertram belonged to a family that had immersed themselves through early Western District settlement to achieve great property and wealth. From Lara, only a gallop away, lay Corio Bay, about 45 miles south-west of Melbourne, where much was owed to Armytage pioneering and industry. It was Armytage shepherds and shearers who started wool on its journey to the mills of the northern hemisphere; Armytage employees and contractors who crammed the bales of the well-named golden fleece into Geelong's cavernous bluestone stores; Armytage hands who groomed the horses, polished the brassware and cooked the meals for maybe 50 eager guests.

Armytage money supported local schools, the cricket clubs, churches, footballers, horse racing and polo playing, and the rowers. Their endless paddocks stretched from Geelong to the South Australian border, their mansion homesteads, stables and coaches betokening the crème of a society rich enough to embrace life as they pleased to make it, in an outdoors of sunshine, gum trees and blue skies, where healthy bodies were said to make healthy minds, though in Bertram's case this formula may have failed him.

The foundations of Armytage land and wealth had been achieved in the less than 50 years before Bertram's birth. His great-grandfather, George, who spent part of his young life in Brussels, arrived in Van Dieman's Land (Tasmania), at the age of 22 in 1817, and as a free settler chose a place called Bagdad where his modest sheep run grew to 5000 acres. At the news of larger pastures in western Victoria he sent his sons Thomas and George across Bass Strait with a flock of sheep to begin a squatter's holding of Ingleby on the Barwon River at Winchelsea. They were tough and dangerous times for a new settler and only a fool would go into the bush without a gun. Noting that there were always casualties on both sides, Thomas's partner and his workman met a grisly end when they intruded on the hunting grounds of a local Aboriginal tribe. Thomas died aged 22, but brother George, one year younger, turned to enlarging the flock and expanding the holdings on which they 'squatted'. Soon the very act of 'squatting' was made legally respectable by a government which recognised that income could be extracted from those who first settled the land, and others who purchased when holdings were broken up. In either case, the land was given a firm marketable value which it did not necessarily have before, and it was a bonanza for the squatters.

George, who died in 1862 aged 67 at The Hermitage, his 20-room mansion in Geelong, divided the Armytage land among the surviving male heirs of his family of seven sons and four daughters. Those who shared were George Francis at Ingelby and Murrandara; Charles Henry at Fulham, Mostyn and Mount Sturgeon; Ferdinand Felix at Turkeith and Mooleric; and Frederick William at Wooloomanata. In all, the holdings totalled about 290,000 acres (50,000 hectares) and the sheep numbered in the hundred thousands. Their relationship to the land also grew through the marriage of George's daughters to Western District men – Eliza to J. R. Hopkins of Wormbete; Elizabeth to J. C. Galletly of Elcho; Virginia to George Fairbairn of Windemere, Lara. Though the union of Eliza Armytage to John Hopkins happened 20 years before Bertram was born, through succeeding generations it was this marriage that would determine his membership of the British Antarctic Expedition, and possibly what transpired afterwards at the Melbourne Club.

STUDENT DAYS

Peter, the Geelong guide of encyclopaedic knowledge, took me to view a large Gothic-style building with steep pitched slate roof and greying paint that stands just around the corner from Moorabool Street, which links the city to the river. This, the original Geelong Church of England Grammar School, is where a 12-year-old Bertram, like his brothers and many cousins, came to serious grips with the three R's in a curriculum – academic and spiritual – which mirrored the best of British learning. Subjects which confronted him were spread wide across English, French, Greek, Latin, history, geography, mathematics (trigonometry, conic sections, euclid, algebra) bookkeeping, field surveying, drawing, scripture, music, gymnastics. Sport was the other major component of the school year, and was taken very seriously: not every boy could be expected to possess great intellect, but if he excelled on the playing fields, who would quibble? Bertram, one feels, fitted very comfortably into the latter category. Armed with a Martini Henry rifle and drawn bayonet, he established a reputation as a good shot in the school cadets; he merited a place in the champion cricket and football teams.

Rowing was the other sport for which Bertram showed a natural bent. Rowing was a sport embraced at Geelong, with a 'playing field' that began just down the street where they had a boat club beside the broad flowing Barwon. According to Michael, the school archivist, rowing began seriously in 1881 with the coming from Oxford of James Lister Cuthbertson who, besides classics master was a driving force in getting the boys behind the oars. Incidentally, Michael mentioned, Cuthbertson committed suicide in January 1910, shortly before Bertram took his own life at the Melbourne Club. Supplanted by the college's new school on a much larger site along Corio Bay in 1914, the old building where Peter had taken me stands seemingly empty and somewhat spooky on premium real estate only a few blocks from the city's commercial heart. The worn steps which we climbed no doubt had known Bertram's footfalls among the hundreds of boys who trudged or sprinted up and down their steepness, according to the time of day. Alongside the steps, a metal plaque told us that the structure to which it was attached 'began as part of a quadrangular Gothic building designed for the school's sponsors by Backhouses and Reynolds of Geelong. The school having opened in 1855 at 65–66 Villamanata Street . . . moved in April 1858 to this building whose foundation-stone had been laid on 24 June 1857 by Sir Henry Barkly, Governor of Victoria'.

Under its present-day title of Geelong Grammar, the prestigious school of soaring brick and wide green spaces should ever be respectful of the Armytage name. George, Bertram's grandfather, was one of the school's founding trustees who campaigned for an institution of quality education that would groom their sons, in the tradition of the Church of England, to accept the mantle of management and leadership. George's sixth and seventh sons, Bertram's father and his uncle Felix, were among the 14 boys enrolled on the opening day in 1855. They began, as Michael told me, a family tradition which has seen more than 150 Armytage names on the roll at Geelong.

Boarding school days ended for Bertram in 1885 when his father again leased Como from the peripatetic Caroline. For the next two years a horse and buggy ride would carry him beside the river to St Kilda Road and the bluff bluestone pile that is Melbourne Church of England Grammar School. In the Mitchell Library, I consulted the school's *Liber Melburniensis* of years past and found B. Armytage was student number 1946 in 1886 while other Armytages went by the initials of C. N., G. F., J. M., N. F., O. F. He was listed among those who fought for the British Empire in the South African War and a member of the Shackleton expedition 1907–1909; d. 1910.

After two years at Melbourne, once again Bertram was on the move. By 1887 his trunks were packed and, farewelled by his family at Port Melbourne pier, he was a voyager to the far side of the world, following in the footsteps of other Armytages for whom Jesus College at the University of Cambridge was the peak of learning – and rowing. With him came 19-year-old Ernest De Little, a Geelong school days chum, and another sportsman who won his cricket 'blue' at Cambridge. In the years ahead he would be best man when Bertram waited at the altar of the big church in South Yarra.

CHAPTER 3

THE ROWER

The oars decorating the wall at Como are testimony to Cambridge's jolly boating days. They belong to Bertram's cousin, Norman (Charles Norman), eldest son of Como's owner, and a legendary in the annals of Jesus College who won his 'blue' for rowing Cambridge to victory in the Grand Challenge against Oxford. Bertram's eldest brother, Frederick, was a member of the winning scratch fours in 1880 and at the Henley-on-Thames races in the following year. His second eldest brother, Harry, was captain of a Jesus boat, Boat Club captain in 1884 and cox in the winning first boat at the Grand Challenge at Henley in 1885.

Among this assortment of athletic brothers and cousins, Bertram proved no exception. He was another rugged colonial who would help to speed a Jesus boat across the line. Jess, my London researcher (whose husband has a farmhouse in Kent and boats on the estuary) spoke with Dr F. H. Willmoth, keeper of the Jesus College records. We confirmed B. Armytage's entry to Cambridge in October 1887, on a recommendation from another Jesus man, Dr John Bracebridge Wilson, headmaster at Geelong from 1863 to 1895, who was obviously well aware of the Armytage name.

Alas, Dr Willmoth regretted that Jesus College records were rather sparse for the years before 1890 so no entry could be found for Bertram's academic performance, which might be doing the

18-year-old lad a favour, for neither does Geelong have any such information. As his old Antarctic sledging mate, Professor Edgeworth David, affectionately wrote, he was 'a simple minded fellow' and 'a gallant and loyal friend'.

But of his participation at Cambridge in rowing, there is ample evidence in the *Chanticleer* of 1887–1888, the termy college magazine which Dr Willmoth kindly sent to Jess and which sounds like an extract from *Boys Own Annual*.

At the start of the Lenten term events, Bertram, weighing in at 10 stone 1½ pounds (the heaviest man was 11 stone 3½ pounds) received number 7 position in the first boat. However his opportunity to display the Armytage mettle disappeared when number 4 died at the oars when rowing in the Clare boat. 'The races were, of course, stopped and at the captain's meeting held immediately afterwards, were postponed sine die.'

Victory came to Bertram's crew in the big race. Despite the burden of an injured cox, C. W. Ingles, the First Lent boat for the second time in the annals of the Club carried off the Granta Cup and Medals, and were awarded their oars. 'One more word and we have done with the Lents', continued the *Chanticleer*. 'We hail as a happy omen the increased amount of enthusiasm which was exhibited over these races, more especially by non-rowing members of the College. A large contingent came down and ran over each night with either boat, no doubt by their vociferous cheering stimulating the crews in no small degree'. Cambridge's milleiu of enthusiasm surely must have gripped the young Australian rower. He had heard of the Jesus College spirit from brothers and cousins, and now he was part of it and in a winning boat.

In the next event, the sliding seat trial eights, Fogg-Elliot was again matched against the old rival, W. H. Chitty. Drama intervened when Fogg-Elliot was summoned to make ninth man in the 'Varsity boat at Putney, and Bertram came from Chitty's bow to fill the vacant after thwart. Without wishing in any way to detract from Armytage's merits, a change so late in the day must have told against them. The race needs little description as Chitty's boat won hands down from second station . . . and paddled in winner by about 80 yards'.

Yet within a few months, the champions seemed to have lost their punch. 'The May term of 1888 has, alas! brought anything but glory to the Jesus College Boat Club', lamented the *Chanticleer*. 'Both boats have descended, and, worst of all, have yielded to crews which were really their inferiors in point of pace, but superior to them in point of pluck . . . the quality of oarsmanship was not A1.' However B. Armytage continued to impress for he was allocated bow position in Fogg-Elliot's first boat. The Jesus performance improved and Bertram held his seat on the last two nights of the races. Both crews were much encouraged by the presence of a 'whole Jesus man' at the start of the first night. 'Truly esprit de corps has not died out in Jesus.'

Away from the oars, one wonders if Bertram participated in a debate on the entrance of new age technology to Jesus College. Did he send his parents a copy of the *Chanticleer* which examined the issue:

> We have received a letter advocating the introduction of the telephone into college. This is an age of luxury and idleness, whose handmaid is electricity. Already all the sights and sounds of the world are collected together in London; soon, what with telephones and photographs and telegraphs and phonographs, we shall not have to move outside our own rooms in order to see and hear everything. And yet a telephone sounds nice. 'Its advantages are numerous and obvious,' urges our correspondent, 'and its expense (£10 a year) not formidable. Other colleges have it, why not we?' We might do worse.

One year was Bertram's brief quota at Cambridge. Despite the heady days of rowing, by 1889 he had farewelled the College and made his way home. Was it for the lack of academic record, or to see blue Australian skies again? Perhaps a restlessness that would haunt him in the years ahead was already stirring.

THE FORT

A warm Sunday afternoon is a pleasant time to walk the battlements of Fort Queenscliff as part of a visitors' tour to trace the life of men who guarded the entrance to Port Phillip Bay and the safety of the populace sleeping soundly beyond. Since 1882 the heavy muzzle loaders had pointed toward the turbulent waters of The Rip, waiting for someone to put a taper to the wick, waiting for the invader who never came. These were the colony's front-line defences, we were told, and as I imagined they would be when Bertram first joined Fort Queenscliff as an eager young Lieutenant, clad in a splendid uniform all target-bright in scarlet and blue. In the Fort's museum we could see how they looked, before the bloody lesson of the snipers in South Africa had them change to khaki and instead of the Indian helmet, a soft felt hat with turned-up brim. We gathered around the pride of the Fort, a massive six-inch which on its 'disappearing carriage' slid out of sight when fired, leaving the enemy in utter confusion. Bertram is possibly one of the figures in the photograph, standing stiffly by the gun waiting for the command. What a deafening noise the bang! must have made in the confines of the pit.

At the Easter 1891 training camp two men died at Fort Queenscliff when the unsecured breech block of a six-inch blew back on the gun crew after it was accidentally fired. 'Our shoddy military', raged a local newspaper. 'Are there any other forts in the world mounted with the same rotten guns? Our garrison artillery take their lives literally in their hands, as they never know when a rotten gun will burst.'

To Bertram and his friend, Percy Chirnside, the tragedy underscored the need for improving the colony's defences. For 10 years past, the government had been at full alert to protect Victoria's coast and the port of Melbourne against an enemy (meaning Russian) attack. Guarding the entrance to Port Phillip Bay, the troops of Fort Queenscliff busied themselves in scanning the horizon, polishing buttons, boots and belts, loading and unloading ammunition, marching, signalling, saluting, shouting orders, and occasionally shooting at a target towed 2000 yards offshore to show what they would do to a hostile (Russian) battleship.

The fact that from year to year the enemy failed to materialise was not allowed to dim the fervour of the colonial defenders like Bertram, who comprised a mixture of full-time soldiery and part-time volunteers manning the seven coastal forts and numbering a thousand strong. They adhered to a regular schedule of parades and Easter camps, and attending Captain John Monash's lectures at North Melbourne Barracks on handling the latest weapons – which they didn't have. Instead, the inventive Monash taught them how to fight using a modern breech block he had fashioned from wood.

The lack of adequate weaponry was felt most severely at the half batteries maintained by two of the colony's richest – the Rupertswood Battery of Sir William Clarke at his Sunbury estate, and Andrew Chirnside's at the family's Werribee Park, alongside the Bay. Both owners put their sons in command and invested £2000 a year on the upkeep of their private armies, which the *Age* portrayed as the patriotic action of concerned settlers who were 'among the very few of our wealthy who have recognised any duty to their country in defence of the wealth it has given them'. Nothing was mentioned about being equipped to keep the lower orders in check. Nothing good could be said, either, about the 37 elite officers seconded from the British Army to train the colonial force. The importation of these men, complained the newspaper, 'has been any-thing but a brilliant success . . . These gentlemen prefer to philander about Collins Street and Toorak than attend to the batteries under their command'.

Guns had been part of Bertram's growing up. Pistols, rifles, shot-guns, hunting guns – for the rich, an extension of personal power. How to clean and load them, how to carry, store and secure them, and how to shoot with pinpoint accuracy; it was a drill that had been inseparable from Bertram's life since school days with the Geelong cadets. After 18 months of tasting life in London and

Bertram Armytage, aged 18, and about to leave for Cambridge where he would row in the champion Jesus College boat. COLLECTION OF THE NATIONAL TRUST OF AUSTRALIA (VICTORIA)

Below: The Armytages were among the founders of Geelong Grammar School where the family educated their sons. The original building of 1858 still stands in central Geelong. AUTHOR'S COLLECTION

Top right: In a painting at Como, the two-year-old Bertram Armytage wears a dress with blue ribbons which seems hardly the garb for a future polar explorer. COLLECTION OF THE NATIONAL TRUST OF AUSTRALIA (VICTORIA)

Above: Bertram Armytage was born at Elcho on 29 September 1869. The Gothic-style homestead stands outside Geelong on the Bacchus Marsh road. AUTHOR'S COLLECTION

Top: Como in the 1880s. COLLECTION OF THE NATIONAL TRUST OF AUSTRALIA (VICTORIA)

Middle: A plaque in Collins Street recalls the history of one of Victoria's oldest and most exclusive clubs. The Armytage males were among its prominent 19th-century members. AUTHOR'S COLLECTION

Above: The Melbourne Club in the 1890s at the fashionable eastern end of Collins Street. Room 24 looked out from the first floor. PICTURES COLLECTION, STATE LIBRARY OF VICTORIA

Top far left: Como, the former Armytage mansion in South Yarra, is now a property of the National Trust in Victoria. Charles Armytage, Bertram's uncle, purchased the property in 1864 for £14,000. AUTHOR'S COLLECTION

Bottom far left: The Armytage family enjoying the front garden at Como where Bertram lived during the 1880s and often visited to see his cousins. It also saw his funeral leave.
COLLECTION OF THE NATIONAL TRUST OF AUSTRALIA (VICTORIA)

Left: 'I am a sportsman,' Bertram boasted. Antlers displayed at Como are evidence of his marksmanship.
UNIVERSITY OF MELBOURNE ARCHIVES

Below: The Armytage coat of arms – 'Always prepared'.
AUTHOR'S COLLECTION

Visitors came to Wooloomanatta to view 'the most important private collection of
modern paintings' in Victoria. However the Armytage art dramatically lost value in the
1890s crash. COLLECTION OF THE NATIONAL TRUST OF AUSTRALIA (VICTORIA)

Inset: Frederick William, sixth son of George Armytage, and one of the founders of the
family fortune. Frederick was a successful pastoralist and businessman; Bertram was
the youngest of his four sons. STATE LIBRARY OF VICTORIA

Top: The Armytage family in high spirits leaving for the Melbourne Cup. Bertram, in military uniform, stands to the right. UNIVERSITY OF MELBOURNE ARCHIVES

Above: Built by his father in 1869 from basalt quarried on site at Lara, the 30-room Wooloomanatta was Bertram's country home. AUTHOR'S COLLECTION

John Percy Chirnside, otherwise known as 'Pursey' to the locals because of his donations to worthy causes. A member of one of Victoria's richest families, Percy commanded the 'half battery' at Werribee Park; his friend Bertram was a fellow officer. STATE LIBRARY OF VICTORIA

Now a hotel resort, the Chirnside mansion of Werribee Park once fielded its own artillery company costing £2000 a year to maintain. PICTURES COLLECTION, STATE LIBRARY OF VICTORIA

JUMPING. — HORSE ARTILLERY - CHIRNSIDE'S

Top: Galloping and shooting were the rewards for those who could afford a part-time officer's life in the colonial military. STATE LIBRARY OF VICTORIA

Above: Entry to London's Cavalry Club came with Bertram's rank in the 6th Dragoon Guards. It also opened many doors to England's hunting estates. AUSTRALIAN ANTARCTIC DIVISION

THE RETURN — HORSE ARTILLERY — CLARKE'S.

Top left: The public now have access to Fort Queenscliff and its museum displays which include this vintage artillery piece. AUTHOR'S COLLECTION

Left: Appointment as a junior lieutenant in the colonial field artillery brought Bertram to Fort Queenscliff, where the explosion of a six-inch gun at Easter 1891 caused deaths and injuries. PICTURE COLLECTION, STATE LIBRARY OF VICTORIA

Above: The half battery company of Sir Rupert Clarke at Rupertswood was, in a sense, a rival of the Chirnsides in the defence of colonial Victoria. STATE LIBRARY OF VICTORIA

Left: Annie Chirnside of Werribee Park and Toorak — a leader in the Melbourne fashion stakes. WATSON FAMILY ALBUM COLLECTION

Below: Samuel Watson produced some of the colony's finest wool from his 25,000 sheep at Gerogery, near Albury. Their proximity to Melbourne drew the family toward Victorian society rather than travelling Sydney-wards. WATSON FAMILY ALBUM COLLECTION

The Watson sisters from New South Wales married into Melbourne wealth. Anne (right) became Mrs George Chirnside, while her younger sister Blanch ('Bon') wed Bertram Armytage. WATSON FAMILY ALBUM COLLECTION

Inset: Bertram, aged 24, at the time of his marriage to Blanch Watson, 23, in 1895. COMO COLLECTION, NATIONAL TRUST OF VICTORIA

Above: Lieutenant Ernest Shackleton, otherwise 'The Boss', leader of the British Antarctic Expedition (BAE) 1907–1909. AUTHOR'S COLLECTION

A crowd of 30,000 people gathered at Port Lyttelton on New Year's Day, 1908, to watch an overladen *Nimrod* leave New Zealand for Antarctica. MAWSON CENTRE, SOUTH AUSTRALIAN MUSEUM

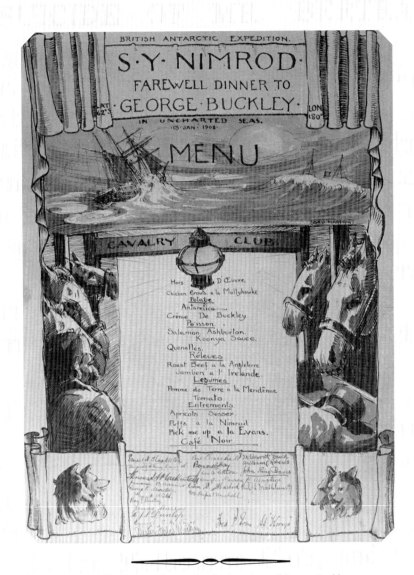

The menu prepared by George Marston for the departure of George Buckley,
a New Zealand sheep farmer who 'came for the ride' until the pack ice.

Cambridge, he had returned to help in managing his father's properties acknowledging he was no academic and indulging in his
favoured pastimes of horse riding and hunting, whether the quarry
be on foot or wing. In his outdoor garb of plus-fours, matching
shooting jacket and Norfolk cap he would cut an elegant figure,
especially on the estates of old England to which the Armytage
males made regular pilgrimages.

Maybe to satisfy a boyish love of the gun, his ambition turned to
the largest gun of all – the artillery, for which one needed to be a
soldier or, as befitted an Armytage, an officer. And not necessarily
a paid one, meaning that he could enjoy the best of both his worlds,
the big guns at Fort Queenscliff and the Chirnside's half battery at
the Park.

Joining the Field Artillery Brigade in September 1889, Bertram
reached the rank of a reserve junior lieutenant within six months.
With a recommendation from Percy Chirnside, his enthusiasm was
later rewarded with a place in the much-coveted artillery short
course for promising officers, and on four weeks' full pay. In the signalling class he learned to use the heliograph, a skill which would
prove of life-or-death value when in, as he later called it, 'a rather
serious position' in Antarctica.

Bertram had much in common with George and Percy: land,
money, horses and hunting, and a place on the Government House
invitation list; and in the case of younger brother Percy, the guns. A
few hours' gallop through the bush would take Bertram to the
Chirnside mansion where the muzzle loaders pointed across the
Bay and a dozen fine chestnut mounts waited in the stable. When
Percy, who commanded the half battery, announced in September
1890 that he had been invited to further his military career with the
Royal Regiment of Artillery at Woolwich and Aldershot, Bertram
was his nominee to command the guns.

For the 21-year-old lieutenant, a moment of glory came in
Melbourne on 24 May 1891 when the colony celebrated Queen
Victoria's 71st birthday. The day began with a 21-gun salute at

noon to honour a monarch who had come to the throne only three years after the first Armytage sailed across Bass Strait. Regaled in the scarlet and blue, Bertram rode in procession at the head of his Permanent Artillery Contingent, with their head-tossing chestnuts and polished gun carriages. They began at the Haymarket and to the beat of brass bands stretched in a half-mile column down Swanston Street, across the Yarra Bridge and along St Kilda Road to the Albert Park parade ground where 5300 men on boot and stirrup assembled for the largest military pageant the city had witnessed.

Bertram spent a year directing the world of mock warfare until Percy returned from Aldershot, only to find the Russian scare had officially ended, or so the government decreed. Despite the promises of several years before, Sir William and the Chirnsides were informed that money no longer would be spent on replacing their half batteries. In truth, the decree was of a government strapped for cash in the economic crisis of the 1890s; a drought was laying waste to crops and livestock; Melbourne shuddered 'in a panic of unbelief' as banks closed their doors, wages were cut, hours reduced, sackings and evictions enforced. Amid the worst of depressions, who needed the Russians?

George Chirnside, ever a realist and with a vision of transforming his Werribee Park into a model agricultural estate, had no patience with hopeless causes, especially in the face of falling wool prices. He quickly set about dismantling the battery, dispersing the classic chestnuts, clearing the stables to house ploughs and steam pumps, and converting the orderly room into a mechanised butter factory. Percy deplored the waste of his time spent at Aldershot and resolved to fight on another front, that of a Member of Parliament. He won the electorate of Grant that had been vacated by Bertram's brother, Harry, and took his seat as an independent in the Legislative Assembly. All of which left Bertram without a war to fight, or an enemy to repulse.

Bertram remained a member of the Horse Artillery, still able to stride the battlements at Fort Queenscliff and fire a canon or two.

But his was a demoralised force, not surprising when among the ranks many of his less fortunate comrades belonged to that other world which knew not where their next ten shillings would come from, or who would pay the rent. Though his reputation was that of a kind young man, sympathetic to deserving causes, other men's anguish belonged on a different planet. He might know the irritation of a lost ambition and increasingly wonder where life would take him, but his bank balance, his bed and his wardrobe suffered no pain. Anyhow his fortune had taken an unexpected turn, for if the Chirnsides had lost the half battery, artillery of another sort was about to bring him within firing range of cupid's bow.

CHAPTER 4

THE BRIDEGROOM

The young male Chirnsides inherited a fortune from Andrew, their father, and his bachelor brother Thomas who, despite wealth and property, ended his life in 1887 with a pistol shot while in a fit of depression. The Chirnside story much paralleled that of the Armytage – forebears migrating from England, seizing the early opportunity to graze thousands of sheep on the wide open plains of the Western District and in profiting from the golden fleece, extending their holdings, building a grand house and, in a brave extension of Western civilisation, embracing a life befitting gentlemen of means. Upon Andrew's death in 1890, the great estate was ready for breaking apart – of which more later.

Five years before his inheritance, George Chirnside wed Annie Watson in one of the most expensive weddings of Marvellous Melbourne's high-spending 1880s.* Annie Chirnside's younger sister, Blanch, was a bridesmaid and became a guest at Point Cooke, their bluestone home alongside Werribee Park. Through the Chirnside connection, inevitably Bertram and Blanch would meet,

---

* The 1880s saw Melbourne's building boom and the introduction of electric power, sewerage, the telephone exchange and cable trams, and direct rail communication with Sydney and Adelaide. In 1891 Melbourne's population was 491,000 and Sydney's 383,000.

neither encumbered by serious liaisons, and highly eligible for the marriage stakes.

In maturity, Bertram had lost none of his boyishness and athletic enthusiasms. He was neat featured, well-built and, especially when clad in his artillery officer's uniform, had in Victorian terms all the hallmarks – and an Armytage at that – of a 'good catch'. Blanch, like her sister, would be regarded as more handsome than pretty, but she was slim, dark haired and under Annie's tutelage dressed expensively. Frequently she and Bertram were partnered at Annie's dinners and parties. Major social events they attended were cousins George Armytage's marriage in Toorak to Amelia Tyler with the reception at Clendon, the Tyler's mansion, and Leila's 'coming out' during the Melbourne Cup season of 1894. Romance was surely in the air; friends must have wondered when the two would make a match of it.

Courtship was inevitably intermittent given Bertram's preoccupations and peregrinations with his military service, horses, hunting and enjoying the male preserve of club life with a background of ocean travel, London and Cambridge. For the rest of it, in Melbourne he had the affectionate friendship of his cousins, Ada, Laura, Leila and Constance at Como; and if he ever visited the 'saddling paddock', otherwise the side bar at the Theatre Royal, we are not aware. Beyond the borders, shearers and bosses were in serious conflict and he would confront the reality of rising unionism among the workers while assisting his father with his properties in outback New South Wales and Queensland. Perhaps in an expression of his unsettled personality, Bertram was slow to go on bended knee. But courtship, as Victorian manners dictated, must have a purpose, and in 1894 when he was 24 and she 23, Blanch and Bertram announced their engagement.

THE WEDDING

Blanch was born at Gerogery Station on 12 July 1870, the third daughter of Samuel Watson whose 24,000 acres and 25,000 sheep produced some of the finest wool in the Southern Riverina of

New South Wales. Known as 'Bon' ('the bonny one', said her father) she grew up knowing about horses and dispatching snakes and quality of the fleece and all the other earthy attributes that would fit a young woman of means to mix with males of the squattocracy. Her mother died when she was aged nine, and six years later her father died, leaving the property to the eldest of his three sons, but ample money to them all. In his later years, Sam Watson installed a manager at Gerogery and moved the family to Wareroonook, another of gold-rich Melbourne's fine residences, where their name would find a slot in the social calendar alongside Armytages and Chirnsides.

Away from the confines of Gerogery's hamlet, Annie the elder sister lost little time in enjoying herself as befitted the daughter of a wealthy pastoralist. Her marriage to George Chirnside at Christ Church, South Yarra, on 28 November 1888 put the seal on her place in society. Annie and Blanch appear to be the two sisters who were drawn together by all the glitter that Melbourne had to offer, whereas other family members returned to marry and work the land around Gerogery. On their sometime visits to the old home, an hour's buggy ride would take them back to the busy border town around which their growing up had revolved. The saying went that Albury was well aware when the Watson women were in town, as they swirled down Dean Street, watched for their dress style, their hair-do and hat, and who they greeted and who they didn't. Staff at Mates department store brought out their best and brightest for this pair of big spenders, but privately regarded them as a rather painful 'pair of snobs'.

For many of these memories I am indebted to Carleen, an elegant and gracious lady, whom I visited on pilgrimages to the modern city of Albury and the countryside beyond where the landmark of Table Top Mountain stands as a background to the Watson's fertile land.

Once installed as wife to George Chirnside, Annie rapidly left her imprint on a Melbourne society of the landed rich. Her dinner parties, race day picnics and receptions were lavish and expensive, and the champagne flowed with abandon. Indeed, Annie became noted for the quality of a liquor cabinet which was never empty; during her parties at Menzies Hotel, the waiters knew to reserve her a brandy crusta discreetly behind the curtain. If the unwritten rule of masculine power suggested that beautiful women made the ideal wives of the rich, it followed that the same rich and beautiful women should spare no expense in grooming themselves as their husbands would have society see them. So if Annie would be admired for her classy gowns and magnificent jewellery, her house must be of the same quality. Without much argument she was able to move the Chirnsides from Werribee's dreary flat lands to the top-drawer Melbourne suburb of Toorak by the Yarra, where neighbours only lived in mansions crowned with flag-fluttering towers (like Government House) embedded in huge gardens and hired footmen for their coaches. Built by the proceeds of wool, gold or property, or maybe all three, these grand houses of the curving, gravelled drives, gargoyles and stables, and drawing rooms stuffed with drapes and frills, brass ornaments and artless prints, were known by names such as Arooma, Laluma, Kyeamba, Ottawa; in the march of time most have disappeared though quiet avenues and crescents recall their names.

Following society's pattern of renting for a time while deciding where to build the next mansion, the Chirnsides leased massive Illawarra with its 25 huge rooms and ballroom, and surrounding two-and-a-half acres complete with tennis court and resident cow. Next they settled upon an address more suited to Annie's sophisticated tastes with wide verandahs, tower and many chimneys sprawled behind garden and hedge close to where Orrong Road meets Toorak Road. Here in a choice corner of the very best suburb was Mont Alto, another player in Bertram's unfolding life. I walked the discreet and leafy streets of this prime corner of Toorak just to sample the sky and clouds that framed Bertram and his bride on their wedding day. Nothing else is left. The grand house where they danced, toasted and made speeches long ago fell to the demolisher's hammer; all that remains is Montalto Avenue, enclosing priceless real estate.

The headquarters of the Victorian Historical Society in A'Beckett Street, Melbourne, contains fascinating literature on the manners of those who dwelt in big houses, especially in the etiquette of the calling card, a little square of cardboard that sought to replay the manners of an old England which probably their forebears never could afford. The cult of the calling card required the wife of a couple who had been entertained to thank host and hostess by returning with her own card next day which maybe she, or more likely her footman, left with the housemaid or on a silver tray, or if the hostess advertised she was 'at home' on a specified afternoon (usually a Wednesday), maybe over a cup of tea, but staying only briefly. Leaving the card met an accepted society obligation; for a newcomer it hopefully gained entry to the social circuit – yet with the risk, if judged as being not quite 'naice' (usually meaning in trade), of never again receiving a Toorak invitation.

Annie perhaps preferred to keep her calling cards busy, for nature did not encourage her role as a Chirnside mother; if George wished for a son, they were disappointed in the early deaths of two infants, one a male; the third, a girl, did survive to be her father's constant companion, in growing up fulfilling the role, as some would say, of the son he didn't have.

When Bertram and Blanch announced their wedding date of 30 January 1895, Annie determined that her young sister's marriage would lack for nothing less than her own to George Chirnside, when they transformed the church into 'a perfumed garden'. It would be the same society church, same exclusive guest list, same no-expense-spared party afterwards. Because the Watson seniors were dead, George and Annie issued the invitations to Christ Church, South Yarra, and the reception at Mont Alto, where Blanch had been living. Jean, my Melbourne researcher, spent hours in the State Library of Victoria tracing the nuptials in *Table Talk*, the bible of Melbourne's upper-crust doings.

By three o'clock on that mid-summer afternoon, the road outside the church filled with carriages and their horsemen and a crowd gathered along the driveway of the tall-spired edifice that, short of St Paul's Cathedral, was the Church of England's most coveted Melbourne address. 'Christ Church, South Yarra, presented a very brilliant scene on Wednesday afternoon', began the report in *Table Talk* of 1 February 1895 which, including the list of presents, spilled over a broad-sheet page. After noting the 'large assemblage of onlookers pressed forward on all sides awaiting a view of the bridal party passing' it continued:

> The decorations of the church consisted of fine palms, and other pot plants, arranged on the pulpit and the reading desk, whilst luxuriant palms and bamboos were banked up on the chancel steps, and marked off the choir seats. Shortly before four o'clock, the organist Mr Percival played the wedding hymn – 'The voice that breathed o'er Eden' – shortly after which the bridal party arrived. The bride entered on the arm of her brother-in-law, Mr. George Chirnside, who subsequently gave her away. The bride-groom's bestman was Ernest De Little (of Camperdown). The service was full choral, Mr. Percival presiding at the organ. The officiating clergymen were the Reverend Horace Tucker (of Christ Church), and the Reverend W. H. Percival (of Lara).
>
> The bride's costume was highly original and very picturesque. It was composed of ivory duchesse satin, over which was draped very fine white tulle, with a tucked skirt and a prettily arranged bodice veiled with tulle; and a court train of ivory duchesse satin draped from the left shoulder. The collar was of the Pompadour style, and fastened with a handsome turquoise heart set in diamonds (the gift of Mrs George Chirnside). She carried a hand-some shower bouquet of romneyas, with white satin loops and streamers. The bridesmaids were all dressed alike, and caused general admiration, in picturesque gowns of a lovely shade of blue marquise satin.

At the conclusion of the ceremony the onlookers scrambled for points of vantage, and hundreds of heads protruded from behind pillars and every accessible point to have a view of the bridal party. The bride who is familiarly known among a great number as 'the bonny one,' and is a general favourite, looked remarkably pretty, whilst the appearance of the bridegroom was very youthful. Amongst the spectators at the church were Mrs. Rupert Clarke and many other society favourites, whose mourning prevented them accepting invitations to the festivities.

A procession of carriages carried the wedding party the short distance along Orrong Road to the big house adorned with coloured lanterns where George and Annie awaited the guests.

At 'Montalto' the scene was very brilliant. Mr & Mrs George Chirnside received the guests at the hall entrance. The rooms were artistically decorated, pot-plants and a choice collection of white blossoms being used in the floral designs. The bride received in the drawing-room which looked very gay and picturesque. After the reception a wedding tea was served in a marquee on the lawn, immediately in front of the hall door.

The tables were profusely adorned with white flowers, white romneyas (favourites of the bride) being most liberally used. Mrs George Chirnside, who sustained her reputation on this occasion of being one of the most charming matrons in Melbourne, was very handsomely dressed in a gown of eau de nil crepe de chine, trimmed with Point Dear' Esprit, having a full bodice, and a box pleat of satin down the back, and large picture sleeves, finished with cuffs of Point Dear' Esprit. A gold embroided girdle around the waist gave a finishing touch to a most dainty and becoming toilette. With this was worn small Parisian gold bonnet, relieved with a cherry velvet bow, and a lovely posy of pink roses was carried.

Mr & Mrs Bertram Armytage left on a short honeymoon tour

after six o'clock, and departed amid the hearty congratulations of all present.

The words 'silver' and 'cheque' and 'diamonds' tended to predominate in *Table Talk*'s report of the wedding presents:

> Mr. & Mrs. F. W. Armytage, case silver plate, case of Sevres china, household linen and to bridegroom, cheque. The Countess of Hopetoun, ostrich feather fan. Mr. & Mrs. Fred Armytage, Neapolitan silk shawl. Mrs. Charles Armytage, silver kettle. Mr. George Chirnside, cheque. Mrs. George Chirnside, diamond and turquoise brooch, Mr & Mrs. George Armytage, silver boiler. Lady Clarke, silver lemon squeezer. Mr. & Mrs. P. Chirnside (to bridegroom), silver flask. The Earl of North Esk en tout cas . . .

And so it went on for nearly the column and a half that *Table Talk* devoted to the dining-room scene where tables and trestles groaned beneath the weight of colonial largesse. Bertram gave his bride a pair of curb bangles. From Blanch he received a pair of polo sleeve links. In its social column, *Table Talk* announced that Mr and Mrs Bertram Armytage (nee Watson) 'will, in a fortnight's time, take up their residence at "*Wooloomanata*", Lara, the residence of Mr. Fred Armytage. They will remain at the station for six months and then proceed to Europe'.

In the marriage records of Christ Church, South Yarra, I found entry number 779 for 30 January 1895 with the bridal signatures. Bertram is recorded as 'Bachelor', aged 25, and his residence as the Melbourne Club, Melbourne. His wife is Blanch Dunn Watson, 'Spinster', aged 24, of Montalto, Toorak, Melbourne. Both their parents, Frederick William Armytage and Samuel Watson (dec.) are 'Grazier'. No longer the squattocracy.

One wonders what Percy Chirnside (who gave the bridegroom a silver flask) thought of all the expensive fuss. When he and the beautiful Ethel Mary Fenner were married two years before on

28 February 1893, they opted for a relatively quiet wedding at All Saints, St Kilda, out of deference to the tough times most others in colonial Victoria were enduring.

CHAPTER 5

LOCKING THE GATES

Bertram and his bride returned from their honeymoon to find that civil war had broken out between the Chirnsides. Within a few months of their wedding, the same George Chirnside who had walked Blanch up the aisle was in conflict with his young brother over division of their late father's estate. George, the elder, inherited Werribee Park mansion with its 60 rooms and all its outhouses, gardens, livestock and the fertile 45,000 acres on which it stood. Percy, as younger brother, drew the shorter straw, meaning 35,000 lesser acres on the western side of the intersecting Geelong railway, satisfactory land for sheep farming but compared to Werribee Park's green field, a poor second.

Worse, Percy did not emerge with a house of his own, meaning he had to buy land along the river to build the place of his choice. And when he did complete Werribee Park Manor, his brother took out a court order to prevent the use of the word 'Werribee', meaning Percy had to settle for just The Manor.

Mary, their mother, received life tenancy of the mansion, where she chose to lead the life of a wealthy widow, receiving frequent visits from Percy and his children. However, with George absent at his wife's latest Toorak residence and Percy increasingly occupied in Parliament, life in the bush grew lonely. George, intent on transforming Werribee Park into an agricultural estate, argued that improving the farm had prime call on his inheritance and was reluctant to spend money elsewhere. Mary retreated into a corner of the huge house which she could maintain and keep warm, while many of the vacant rooms were closed. Their mother's isolation exacerbated an already prickly relationship between the brothers, especially worsened in George's abrupt abandonment of Percy's command, the half battery, when the government refused to replace the guns. One day the Geelong line gates (giving access between the two properties, Werribee Park and The Manor), were padlocked, symbolising that family communication had ceased.

Bertram faced the problem of treading a rather tricky tightrope in balancing his loyalty between the two brothers, both of them friends. His wife's sister was married to George Chirnside and she and Annie were the closest of sisters; George had been generous in his kindness to Blanch, for that matter, toward them both.

Though he might be characterised by some as 'a hard man', Bertram understood his brother-in-law's dedication to modernising Werribee Park with the installation of steam pumps, steam ploughing, mechanical separators and refrigerator, as well as refining his herds of Jerseys and Herefords. With rising exports of butter and cheese to London and the Far East, he encouraged his many tenants to profit from making Werribee Park one of the colony's most productive properties.

Bertram's relationship with Percy was one of admiration, bonded in their membership of the officer class and a common interest in protecting Victoria from the foreign invader. He saw the fashion-conscious and handsome Percy as the Chirnside with a social conscience, one known for his charity toward less-fortunate neigh-bours, contributing to building schools and churches, and even financing a military exercise in Easter 1897 when the government was unwilling; at the coronation of King Edward VII he deposited one shilling into bank accounts he opened for every school child in the district. His generosity earned him the local nickname of 'Pursey' – which, apparently, he did not find amusing.

In not wanting to take sides, Bertram perhaps recalled a hostile relationship between the Chirnsides and the Armytages some 20 years before when one accused the other of selling them second-rate sheep but charging first-rate prices. Maybe he was also aware that small misunderstandings could lead to a violent outcome; Thomas Chirnside, the bachelor brother of Andrew, had shot himself at Werribee Park in 1887 under the mistaken belief that he was terminally ill and bankrupt. Fortunately wealth and business preoccupations insulated George and Percy from unnecessary personal contact and, being gentlemen, for a time they led their separate lives in an aloofness only compromised by the most pressing family matters. Which was fine for Bertram who could deal with his two friends individually without seeming to take sides, and in the city he had recourse to meetings at the Melbourne Club where men knew the decent way to behave.

In a bizarre sense, the Chirnside drama was staged more subtly in the ballrooms of Toorak, at the theatre first nights and the Spring Racing Carnival at Flemington, where Percy's young wife, Ethel, 'a fair English beauty' and the statuesque Annie, vied in a sisterly-in-law stakes that were scored by coiffure, jewellery and the most recent Paris fashion which, at times, seemed the main purpose of their lives.

Thousands of people visit Werribee Park's restored mansion each year, but they come by coach and private car, and pay, not like the chosen thousand or so of Melbourne's A-list of another century who were ferried across the Bay to attend one of the legendary Chirnside garden parties. Crumbling timbers of the old jetty still poke through the waves and, nearby, grapes are grown where Bertram and his chums once drew a bead on the hundreds of assorted deer, foxes, hares, rabbits, quail, partridges and pheasants that Andrew and Thomas had let loose to satisfy a gentleman's urge to go hunting. Decades later, in 1958, I gave a talk at an austere Werribee Park when it had become the Corpus Christi Seminary for student priests of the Melbourne archdiocese. Antarctica was the subject, from where I had just returned from my first visit; probably I spoke about the hut at Cape Royds where Bertram spent the climactic last year of his life. Was his ghost listening?

In the pubs along the waterfront at Geelong, the talk was of Bertie Armytage and one little canoe which he had paddled across the Bay from Port Melbourne, then carried along the street to the Barwon River at South Geelong, made his way downstream to the open sea of Bass Strait, negotiated the hazardous waters of The Rip, and paddled the fragile craft back up the Bay to Melbourne; it amounted to 75 miles of relentless canoeing. At Geelong Grammar they hailed it as the heroic journey of a superb athlete. Others, less high-minded, downed their beer and wondered if the fellow was slightly daft. In a review of a life cut short, Professor Edgeworth David, his sledging companion at Cape Royds, observed that Bertram Armytage 'knew no fear'; just forever wanting to prove himself?

A book held in the Geelong Historical Society's library quotes from an old lady's memory of the young Bertram, even bestowing on him an honorary knighthood:

> Sir Bertram, a friend of all. He had a wooded paddock fenced high in bird wire and imported some beautiful pheasants, glorious plumaged birds, to breed for sport for their friends from Melbourne and overseas.

Colonial governors, titled visitors from England, and a variety of the squattocracy and their ladies were guests at Wooloomanata, some coming for a day on the hour's train journey from Spencer Street, others equipped for a weekend's shooting. Bertram would elect at times to gallop his father's splendid four-in-hand, taking the weekend people to the Monday morning train. Beside him would sit their uniformed coachman, King Billy, who in his dispossession was befriended by the Armytages who had him baptised and named at the Lara church. King Billy struck an upright regal figure in his cream knee breeches, black cut-away coat, bell topper and polished black leggings; he claimed to 'have shaken hands at Wooloomanata with more governors than any other Aborigine in Victoria'.

Bertram resumed his intermittent role of helping to manage the Armytage properties, interrupted by numerous excursions to enjoy the role, as he liked to boast, of 'I am a sportsman'; and trophies presented to the Melbourne Club as proof of his deadly aim. A year into the married state, he proved to be no reformed stay-at-home which probably accorded with Blanch's expectations of a world in which she had grown up, the male-dominated squattocracy. She was wed to a man described to the world at large within a few years as 'a most reticent man, shy and diffident and subject to all kinds of varying moods . . . though a charming man personally, there was always a trace of eccentricity about him. He loved to do things which other men feared'.

Physical fitness was almost a mania. That he was of average height and build did not count; as with rowing, riding, marksmanship and his new enthusiasm for cycling, it was the excellence of the sportsman-athlete that mattered. For both parties, it was a lifestyle that did not seem to reserve much time for encountering the normal ways of the married state. The final years of the 19th century ticked away and Blanch had not fallen pregnant, perhaps, rather than due to Bertram's perambulations, an acknowledgement that women need not be condemned to a life of serial child-bearing. Contraception was now a quasi-respectable subject to discuss with the doctor. Or in Bertram's dedication to physical fitness, was there an absence of the sex drive?

'Why did he do it?' Blanch wrote, after his death, maybe a question that contains its own answer. One may wonder how well did she and her husband really know each other, aside from the society circles in which they mixed and away from the conventions of Victorian manners when a man courted a woman? Annie certainly would counsel her little sister not to be a Wooloomanata stay-at-home, where she was no mistress of the house. Melbourne and its temptations had much to offer. And they could travel together, as they did in 1902 when the entire Chirnside family sailed for London to attend the coronation of Edward VII. Annual voyages to England and the Continent were part of being rich; an almost weekly flotilla of P&O and Orient liners sailed from Port Melbourne, with maybe a court presentation invitation clutched in the purse of those who merited.* Bloated hat boxes and cavernous Saratoga trunks were inseparable from the luggage of a first-class passenger. Luxury cabins offered a travel style that strayed little from the comforts of Toorak. Among the shipboard company, one might trifle with an innocent romance.

The graves of Frederick William Armytage, his wife Mary Susan, and their youngest son, Bertram, are to be found behind the high red-brick wall that encloses Boroondara Cemetery in the heart of Kew, one of Melbourne's preferred inner suburbs. Oddly enough, in pursuing these Melbourne enquiries in the care of family friend Janice, I found that the bed where I lay was but a 15-minute walk from where Bertram's bones lie in a narrow, unkempt grave, marked only by an ordinary headstone which reads 'In Memory of my husband, Bertram Armytage, died March 12, 1910 aged 40'. Nothing about the Boer War, nothing about leading the Western Party in Shackleton's expedition.

The plot rather thickens when we find that Blanch, who survived until 1955 and did not remarry, is buried in the same Armytage soil beside her husband, but without a headstone. Did anyone care for Blanch? (To be certain of her burial, I twice visited the lady in the cemetery office to check that my information was correct. It was.) Further, the Armytages were Church of England (viz Geelong Grammar, Melbourne Grammar, Christ Church etc) yet their graves belong in the Catholic portion of Boroondara, which serves to

---

* Applications for presentation at court were made to the Colonial Office in London. Elaborate formal dress was hired for the Palace ceremonies which were usually held twice before and after Easter.

recall that the 18th-century Armytages lived in Belgium where three of the great aunts were nuns of the Catholic church, including one who founded a new religious order.*

Which makes it worth recalling that one of the Antarctic decorations awarded to Bertram, which you can see in the cabinet at Como, is a medallion from the King of the Belgians. So?

Bertram's father was one of the movers and shakers of colonial Victoria, a cricketer of note, a shire councillor, a horse breeder, donor to the university's Trinity College, city landowner, and respected member of the Melbourne Club. Apart from Wooloomanata's pleasant acres bordering the You Yang slopes to the north of Geelong, his string of properties stretched from the Western District into the neighbouring colonies. Names such as Mossgiel and Nocoleche in New South Wales and, in Queensland, Norley, Bimbra, Gulbertie and Thargomindah were code for the wealth gained from countless thousands of sheep shorn and countless mobs of cattle sent to market. The paralysing drought and depression of the 1890s were estimated to have cost Frederick 250,000 sheep and 90,000 head of cattle, and a lot more anguish besides, but he survived, partly from the fact as early prospering settlers of Victoria, the Armytages had been able to consolidate their resources.

In 1879, together with two partners, Frederick began Australia's frozen meat trade and when SS *Strathleven* sailed for England, most of the lamb carcases in her freezers bore the brand of F. W. Armytage. The Australian Frozen Meat Company was one of the directorates of this pioneer, whose courage gave great impetus to the country's pastoral industry and who, aged 74, died peacefully at Como. The inscription on the marble monument above his grave

---

* Sophie Armytage (b. 1808) in 1832 founded the Belgian religious order of 'Les Filles de la Croix' which spread elsewhere in the Continent and to England and India. Sophie was its head for 50 years and her sisters Fanny and Maria Ann were also superiors of the Order.

reads 'one who never thought ill of any man'. How much did the youngest son live in awe of Frederick's shadow? His father had begun everything which he now enjoyed, he nothing. In comparison he judged himself as adrift, unsettled, searching.

Old Wooloomanata nowadays is very much a private place. A plate affixed to the front gate specifies entry by appointment, which is understandable, considering the historic nature of the property that stands well hidden from traffic along the Bacchus Marsh road. Nevertheless, Peter, my historian guide, was sufficiently emboldened to lift the latch and drive us along a winding track through clumps of eucalypts and by an olive grove until around a corner, staring out across the Corio plains, we met the massive bluestone house. The Armytages lived in great style. Mary Susan, wife and mother, was a Staughton, another colonial family that had prospered from an early entry into wool. She is buried alongside her husband at Kew beneath the simple epitaph of one 'who suffered the privations and dangers of a pioneer's lot patiently'. The memories of a neighbour recalled her as 'a woman of quiet dignity, always anxious for the welfare of those in need'.

Here is where Bertram grew up; where he went off to college, to Cambridge, to war and Antarctica; where he brought his bride, where he pursued his love of hunting, shooting and horses; and where his family heard the bad news. The house, Italianate in style, is long, wide and single storey and contains some 30 rooms. The bluestone blocks were quarried locally and the fine timber brought from Van Diemen's Land, which the Armytages knew well. The three sides of an enclosing verandah are supported on ornate cast-iron pillars. The rear allows for a wide courtyard and a nest of kitchen, laundry and pantries where the 20 servants went about their business. Large stables face into the courtyard; here the shooting parties would sling their guns and mount their horses, and at Woollomanata they had no shortage of quarry in a country where the imported rabbit had risen to plague proportions; a hired team of three men reported 17,000 rabbits trapped in just a few days' work.

Cats were let loose to kill the rabbits, and as breeding went wild, the place became known as 'cat country'.

The lofty ceilinged wing on the western side contained Frederick's billiards room and art gallery, where he hung the fruits of his numerous travels and his shopping from catalogues sent by the London agents. Frequently the exhibition went on loan to Melbourne's nascent National Gallery, housed in the public library. A newspaper critic regarded the Armytage collection 'of modern paintings as the most important assembled in Victoria in the 19th century'. Yet according to Gerard Vaughan, director of the National Gallery of Victoria, the story that the Armytage pictures ultimately found a place in the National Gallery's vaults is a furphy.

In reality, the much-publicised modern paintings came to a rather shameful end when Frederick, in urgent need of funds during the 1890s economic crash to save Norley, his Queensland property, from the banks, packed them off to London to raise eagerly anticipated funds. However the auction at Christies failed to attract the bidders. *La Promenade*, which Frederick had bought for £3500 brought a mere £199 – and that figure set the tone for most of the sale. The market proved utterly false, or had the colonial sheepherder been duped by the art world's smart men? Among all the paintings that disappeared, one wonders what happened to *A Scene in the Arctic Regions* (Wm. Bradford) which depicted two ships beset in the Arctic wastes. On the wall at Wooloomanata, perhaps it had turned young Bertram's imagination towards exploring the polar ice.

Peter introduced me to the present-day owner of Wooloomanata who was hurrying off to care for his olive trees. On learning the purpose of my visit, he acknowledged the Armytage history and that Bertram had lived here. 'Ah, yes,' he said at the end of our brief conversation, 'the son who shot himself in the Melbourne Club when he found his wife was having an affair with that fellow in London.'

CHAPTER 6

THE DRAGOONS

On a wintry 16 August 1900, Bertram Armytage waited at Lara railway station for the three o'clock train that would begin his journey to the South African war. From the *Geelong Advertiser* of 20 August:

> The many friends of Lieut. Bertram Armytage assembled at the Lara railway station on Saturday afternoon to make him a presentation of a handsome pair of field glasses, suitably inscribed. The presentation was made by Ex-Cr Charles Tayler in a neat speech, in which he remarked upon the interest which all the neighbourhood felt in Lieut. Armytage's appointment to the 6th Dragoon Guards, and the assurance they felt in his proving worthy of that splendid and historic regiment. He only echoed the sentiments of all in saying that they wished him a brilliant career, and, in due time, a safe return to his birthplace, covered with honors and renown. Lieutenant Armytage responded to the toast in brief and soldierlike terms, expressive of his thankfulness for the kind expressions used, and the very useful present. The railway officials – Messrs Macarthur (S. M.), and Wishart – had arranged the waiting room very tastefully for the occasion, and had ornamented it with a number of splendid flags and banners designed and lent by Mr. Armstrong, another railway official of Geelong.

No mention is made of Bertram's wife or family attending his departure. Maybe the kisses were exchanged and the goodbyes said at Wooloomanata; maybe Blanch was not pleased that her peripatetic husband of five years had volunteered to take himself off to war; deaths of fine young Australian lads at the hand of the Boers were beginning to appear in the Melbourne papers. Two days later the *Advertiser* reported another Bertram farewell which made Peter, my historian friend (who located these items), wonder if the workers at Wooloomanata were anxious not to be ignored:

> Previous to Lieut. Bertram Armytage's departure to South Africa to join his regiment (6th Dragoon Guards) the station employees on his father's estate (F. W. Armytage) presented him with a silver-mounted leather-cased glass flask and silver cup, for attachment to saddle, suitably inscribed. Mr G. R. Taylor, station manager, acted as spokesman for the donors and testified to the affection and respect in which the young officer and his parents were held by all employed on the estate. Lieut. Armytage acknowledged the gift in feeling terms, and Mrs. F. W. Armytage invited the party making the presentation to a handsome repast in the picture gallery. Mr Hugh Shiels furnished Mr Armytage with a valuable and useful charger (Scotia) his mother having presented him with another (Tasma). A number of people assembled at the Lara station to bid the gallant dragoon God speed and he departed amid flying bunting, musketry salutes, and hearty cheers, accompanied by the good wishes of all the neighbourhood.

At one level, Federation's cause gripped Australia's cities and countryside; at the other, Boer War fever had seized much of the public imagination. An historian with whom I spoke called it 'red coat dreaming': a good thing in going off to battle for the Empire clad in a bright uniform with buttons polished, rifle slung across the shoulder, a brass band in front ordering the step. Impromptu parades, waving the flag, singing 'God Save the Queen' were popular shows of loyalty that needed no explanation, much less a dissecting of the cause of it all. When relief reached the besieged town of Mafeking, partly by an Australian force, in May 1900, the *Age* reported Melbourne streets swarming with 'a dense mass of roaring, cheering and singing humanity'.

Perhaps it was Mafeking and the likes of it that stung Bertram into action. Sorely pressed by a wily enemy, the British Government had issued a call to the colonies – 'mounted men preferred, indispensable that they should be trained and good shots, and supply their own horses'; for officers, theirs should be 'free from blemish, noble in appearance, full of fire and equitable in temper'. Bertram could place a tick against all three for his two splendid mounts. In all, Australia sent 16,137 horses to South Africa and almost as many men to ride them. Some squatters organised teams of volunteers among their stockmen and equipped them with mounts to suit. An insurance company offered one pound a week for life to the first Australian who would win that medal of supreme bravery, the Victoria Cross. Percy Chirnside donated £500 to assist one of the departing Victorian companies.

The fact that the Boers, descendants of South Africa's original Dutch settlers, had taken arms against their colonial masters in the Transvaal and Orange Free State and threatened the Cape Colony might seem like a very distant scuffle, separated, as it was, by the expanse of the Indian Ocean from Australia. But this was Empire stuff, and honour, duty and glory lay in going to fight for the Mother Country. Contingents of bushmen, lancers, mounted rifle men sailed from various city ports, with bright streamers festooned between ship and shore, strains of 'Land of Hope and Glory' and 'Rule Britannia' fading in full patriotic voice from the farewelling crowds. The Boers would harbour a particular hostility for these Australians, in a sense viewed as sons of the soil like themselves with whom they had no quarrel, yet who had come across the sea to stab them in the back.

But Bertram was not to be one of these enemies; he was a Carabinier, a cavalryman in an elite and historic British regiment who had earned a Boer hatred all of their own. He was a 6th Dragoon Guard; reputedly the best heavy cavalry unit in the British Army.

A visit to Geelong Grammar takes you, as it did for me, along Biddlecombe Avenue to the front gate of this well-endowed and impressive school. John Biddlecombe was a generous benefactor of Geelong Grammar – check the plaque on the chapel wall. In the Boxer Rebellion of 1896 he commanded a warship of the Victorian Naval Brigade. He married into old squattocracy money, husband of Janet Russell, of Golf Hill, a member of another prominent Western District family which would make him the Armytage's friend. Biddlecombe, Norfolk born, was in the 6th Dragoons and his were the connections that enabled Bertram, in the eccentricity of his desire to do something different, to gain acceptance into a British cavalry unit where, normally, one had to be 'invited' to join. Bertram's own career record – Cambridge and Jesus College rowing, the horse artillery, excellence at riding and marksmanship and inde-pendent means – gave him the right credentials. Eligible for London's Cavalry Club and frequent visitor to the great hunting estates, he was known to the right people.

More so, he could afford the Dragoons which did not come cheap. Apart from the purchase of two mounts, the outfitting expenses in London, according to a fellow officer's list, included 'scarlet mess kit, three drill tunics from Jones Chalk and Dawson; from Huntsman three pairs of uniform breeches, three white for polo, a cloak, two pairs of overalls from Tautz, three pairs of boots from Maxwells'.

By the time Lieutenant Armytage reached his Dragoon unit late in 1900, the war had descended to a punishing guerrilla campaign waged by scruffy, bearded men who ambushed the marching columns of red-coated Britishers, looted their equipment, wrecked the railways and on horseback melted into the dust of the veldt ahead of retribution. Though the general staff believed the Boers could not survive into the new year, the reverse was unhappily true. Reinforcements from Britain and volunteers (but only white men need apply) from the colonies were summoned by the thousands.

With the retirement of the elderly Lord Roberts, command went to Major General Lord Kitchener, an Empire hero. Kitchener quickly began to reorganise the fighting. Khaki took the place of red, rifles instead of lances, slouch hats instead of helmets, infantrymen put on horseback. More fundamental to his strategy, the isolated outposts were removed to a chain of fortified block-houses, patrols concentrated on the vulnerable railways, night marches made into hostile territory to play the enemy's game of surprise attack. Even more sweeping was his ruthless policy of scorching the earth where the burghers lived and worked, and building concentration camps to hold their families and others who might support them.

The horsemanship and daring tactics of Australian volunteers won the reluctant admiration of British cavalry officers. The Australians, said one soldier, showed the British regulars 'how to scout, how to take cover, how to ride, how to shoot, how – in short – to play this particular game as it should be played'.

Crowds gathered to read the war news from South Africa pinned to bulletin boards outside the city newspapers. Friends of Bertram would watch in dismay as names on the casualty list embraced the landed gentry known to them all: young Noel Calvert, son of John and Margaret Calvert of Irrawarra Station, near Colac, his mother a daughter of Andrew Chirnside; Edgar Robertson, only son of John and Sarah Robertson of Cororooke in the Western District; Keith Mackellar, aged 20 and of fine physique, the poet Dorothea Mackellar was his sister. Further afield, the 17-year-old Anthony Forrest, a son of the famous Western Australian exploring family, dead within a few days of his first action.

By the start of 1902, though the Boers still had an estimated 25,000 men under arms, through sheer weight of opposing numbers and Kitchener's revised field tactics, their resistance gradually crumbled. Faced with the horror of a countryside stripped of food, their farmhouses destroyed, families herded away, safe refuges and escape routes denied, surprise attacks on sleeping camps, groups of burghers began to disappear, others telling their leaders, even as attacks continued, that the game was up.

On 31 May a cease fire – the Peace of Vereeniging – was signed and the Boers surrendered their arms. Across the two years and eight months of fighting, Britain had poured 450,000 men into South Africa, half of them in the front line, with a death roll numbering 5774 men and 22,829 wounded; ironically more were lost from illness than gunfire. Among the Empire's volunteer forces, Australia contributed 16,175 men and of these, 514 died. From a force of some 80,000 men, the Boers lost more than 4000 killed while 32,000 were in prison camps and 110,000 in concentration camps; some as far distant as Ceylon. Illness in the unhygienic camps took 20,000 lives.

What Bertram did in the war is lost to us. This reticent man either left no record, or his diary perished in the great bushfire. We do know that the 6th Dragoons had already been in action for a year or more when he joined them in South Africa. We know that under the command of Major General John French they marched, scouted and skirmished across the veldt in pursuit of the elusive foe. The Dragoons' front column lancers were most feared by the Boers in close combat, and in return the enemy was said to give no quarter when a lancer fell into their hands.

The 6th Dragoons archives have nothing to say. Jess, my agent, contacted Colonel Roger Binks, regimental secretary of The Royal Scots Dragoon Guards, Home Headquarters, The Castle, Edinburgh. 'I should first explain that our holding of personal records is very limited,' he replied. 'We do hold regimental archives but these, prior to World War Two are very limited . . . sadly we have nothing before 1914. I can only suggest that you write to the National Archives . . .' Jess then reported that National Archives held service papers for regular soldiers of the Dragoons serving during the Boer War, but not those of officers. No list for Lieutenant B. Armytage receiving an Army pension but officers with private incomes rarely claimed a pension. No Armytage listed in the regimental casualty lists.

Somewhere on the veldt another tragic polar figure was also fighting the Boers. Captain Lawrence 'Soldier' Oates, the crippled man who crawled from Scott's tent with the famous last words 'I am just going outside and may be some time', had much in common with Bertram. Both were from wealthy families. Oates, an old Etonian, belonged to the landed gentry, found his pleasure in hunting, horse riding, shooting and sailing. Both were cavalry men – Oates, an officer in the Inniskilling Dragoons* and during the South African war suffered a bullet wound in the thigh which bequeathed him a slight limp.

Oates never married though he once courted a girl. He belonged to an officer class that affected suspicion and indifference towards marriage ('a soldier has no business to be wed', was one motto) and expended their aristocratic energies on the great outdoors and brandy in the mess. Somewhere in this, do we sense a resonance with Bertram? To escape the boredom of peacetime Army life, Oates joined the British Antarctic Expedition of 1910–1912 and was placed in charge of the Manchurian ponies and, as with Bertram, all were lost. Both Bertram and Oates died at their own hands; for the badly frost-bitten 'Soldier' it was by stumbling into the blizzard rather than delay his starving companions. The date was 17 March 1912, two years and five days after Bertram fired the fatal shot. Did the two ever meet?

In the little glass cabinet on the wall at Como I found the only record of Bertram's war. Two medals with ribbons, side by side. One awarded by Queen Victoria towards the close of her reign: the Queen's South African Medal, issued on 1 April 1901, with three

---

* The Inniskilling Dragoons were founded in 1751. Bertram's 6th Dragoon Guards (The Carabiniers) were an older regiment from 1685.

clasps for service in the Cape Colony, Orange Free State and Transvaal. The second with two clasps is awarded by the new sovereign, King Edward VII on 1 February 1902, saying simply, South Africa 1901 and 1902. Two small metal discs and striped ribbons found near the body in room 24 of the Melbourne Club. Such is our evidence of Bertram's fight against the Boers.

The Australian War Memorial in Canberra has a telegraphic message from the Cape Colony District Commander advising that Lieutenant B. Armytage, 6th Dragoon Guards, left Cape Town for Melbourne aboard SS *Yarrawonga* on 18 July 1902. But did he remain in Melbourne? The King's Medal was awarded in Bangladore which suggests he returned to a new posting, though I surmise that maybe it was tiger hunting and not the Guards that gave India its attraction.

Once peace had broken out, however, life with the Dragoons and the need for purchasing replacement mounts, his own having long since died, and spending an annual £600 on feed, uniforms and weaponry must have lost their appeal. Bertram resigned his commission and returned to Wooloomanata and Blanch. One also wonders whether he had enough of life in a British cavalry regiment where the officer class were apt to regard colonials with a supercilious disdain. Probably he survived without too much difficulty. His wealth eschewed the need for pay or pension; his time at Cambridge, his very physical fitness and expertise with horse and rifle, not to speak of his familiarity with London and the Cavalry Club*, all groomed him well for life among the officer class. Possibly he could be portrayed as 'more British than the British', suggested in his manner of exclaiming 'What! What!' at the end of a sentence. It was a habit that would score him an amount of derision in the great adventure to come.

---

* Records of the now Cavalry and Guards Club, according to Secretary David Cowdrey, list 'Armytage B., Lieut., late The Carabiniers' elected to membership in 1902. His name appeared in the Members Book of 1908 but not thereafter.

CHAPTER 7

AUSTRALIA CONTRIBUTES

Friday, 13 December 1907 was no unlucky day for Antarctic exploration. Prime Minister Alfred Deakin rose to his feet in the young Commonwealth's temporary legislative headquarters in Parliament House, Melbourne, to move:

> That this House authorises the Government to advance a sum not exceeding £5000 for the purpose of supplying the necessary equipment to the Antarctic expedition about to proceed to the South Pole.

Deakin prefaced his motion to speak of 'a novel proposal' which had been in his mind during the past week and of a letter he had received two days before from Professor David of Sydney, 'a well known scientific man who is about to accompany the expedition under Lieutenant Shackleton to the South Pole'.

'Owing to losses sustained by others,' Deakin continued,

> who had tentatively promised to contribute, the expedition is short by £5000 of the amount necessary to enable it to obtain a full supply of stores and equipment for its stay in the Antarctic regions, probably, for three years. Although the scientific information to be obtained is of universal value, yet it has a special value

to Australia, because of the greater knowledge of meteorology which it promises, and because if there are any economic possibilities in those Antarctic lands, Australia will probably be the country which will most directly benefit.

Under these circumstances, since the expedition has awakened world-wide interest, and will be one of the best equipped ever dispatched on a mission of danger of this kind, I venture to ask honourable members to give the government authority to advance a sum not exceeding £5000 for the purpose of completely equipping it. The men who are risking their lives in the expedition have already promised to give a considerable share of the scientific specimens – the flora and fauna – which they may gather, to the museums of Australia.

Opposition leader, Andrew Fisher, voiced Labor's acceptance of the motion. Joseph Cook, leader of the other wing of the conservative party, weighed in with his view that:

we owe a duty to ourselves and to posterity to explore the Antarctic regions. From a scientific and, indeed, every point of view, it is our obligation to do what we can to make known all that lies hidden in that mysterious land. I support the motion most cordially. I sincerely hope that the expedition may prove an abundant and abiding success.

Amid the Votes and Proceedings of Federal Parliament (ordered by the House to be printed on that same happy date) you can read, as I did in the Mitchell Library, Professor Edgeworth David's letter that triggered such concord between the government and opposition. 'I have the honour on behalf of Lieutenant Shackleton,' he began, 'whose expedition I am accompanying to the Antarctic regions, to appeal to you as Prime Minister of the Commonwealth of Australia, for financial assistance to this important expedition, led by Lieutenant Shackleton.'

The Welsh-born David, a skilled politician from academia's hallowed halls and a consummate networker, had his way with words:

> The Antarctic is of prime interest to Australia. It has much bearing on our weather and is a possible source of valuable minerals. Weather and magnetic studies will be of practical value to Australia. We cannot afford to neglect our nearest neighbour, our white sister. It is possible that minerals could be discovered of commercial value. Lieutenant Shackleton is taking on his staff representatives from various parts of Australia who will share in the scientific and other work of this important expedition.

The last sentence expressed more hope than fact, but David had made his point. This man of unlimited energy and initiative would open the way for Australia's entry into the age of Antarctic science.

Shackleton (otherwise 'The Boss') at this stage was no figure of world renown as would come within a decade. The extraordinary adventure of his ship *Endurance*, beset in the Weddell Sea pack, the evacuation without loss of 28 men to desolate Elephant Island, and his heroic open-boat voyage to South Georgia all lay in the future. In 1907, Australia knew Shackleton as a 33-year-old merchant marine officer of Anglo-Irish descent who had been a member of the 1901–1904 National Antarctic Expedition (otherwise, in the name of their ship, 'the Discovery' expedition). He had accompanied Captain Scott and Dr Wilson on the longest sledging trek yet made into Antarctica. At the close of the first year, Scott had shipped him home as physically unfit for further Antarctic duty; that was an unjust sentence, it was said, for which he never forgave his leader. Intent on retrieving his reputation as a polar explorer, he had spent the past three years in assembling the privately financed British Antarctic Expedition (the 'BAE'), purchasing a decrepit Norwegian sealer and defying the sceptics of the Royal Geographical

Society. King Edward VII and Queen Alexandria had even come aboard his little *Nimrod* during the Cowes regatta to bid him and his men farewell. What is more, the Queen had presented him with a flag to take to the South Pole. That was a recommendation good enough for Australia.

Edgeworth David had corresponded with Shackleton in London, knew of the shortfall in expedition funds, and now had delivered. For Shackleton the cup overfloweth. The £5000 (New Zealand added £1000) enabled him to purchase extra stores and, even more importantly, gain his expedition a scientific standing that would confound the critics. Thanks to David's initiative Shackleton was able to engage three men from Australia to boost his Shore Party to 15 men. One was David himself, who had already asked to make the return voyage on *Nimrod*; the second was David's brilliant ex-pupil, now a lecturer at the University of Adelaide, the 25-year-old Douglas Mawson. The third was no scientist, yet a willing hand, Bertram Armytage.

Birth Notice
At Alloquin, 12 Williams Rd., Prahran, 6 September, 1906:
Armytage. To Bertram and Blanch, a daughter, Mary Staughton. Mother and baby both well.

Various Armytage, Staughton and Watson women would share a little smile of relief, knowing how Blanch's sister, Annie Chirnside, had lost two of her three children in infancy. The arrival of a healthy daughter seemed to signal that Bertram had retired from his wanderings and returned to the marriage bed, no longer a career cavalry officer and with no more wars to fight. Now at the age of 35, he could find, if he wished, the comforts and stability of squattocracy writ large in his father's estate at Wooloomanata. Melbourne was within easy reach, offering him the hospitality of the Club and with friends sharing his dedication to horseflesh and hunting; and on frequent visits to Como, enjoying the hospitality of cousins Ada, Constance*, Laura and Leila – especially Leila, the youngest, who was outgoing and interested in the world around her, when other rich young women were sometimes groomed to be passive and less informed.

Blanch's name is missing from this recitation, a wife much accustomed to an episodic marriage. Perhaps this is why in the birth certificate she gives her address as Point Cooke while her husband's is at Lara. Motherhood surely offered Blanch an extra dimension to her days, but nurses and nannies were also on call to ensure life did not lack for enjoyment. Especially did she remember her visit, with the entire Chirnside entourage, to the coronation of Edward VII, and the delights that the London season had in store.

If Bertram wanted a point of reference for where life was not taking him he had in Frederick, Harry and Frank three brothers who fitted well into the Armytage mould as men of substance**. Fred, nine years his senior, had returned the Armytages to Tasmania as a prosperous and influential pastoralist along the Tamar River. Another champion of physical fitness, he went to Jesus College and won his oars. While Bertram was fighting the Boers, Fred rowed in a solo and unaccompanied nine-hour marathon, from Geelong to Melbourne's Princes Bridge, paddling a canoe of his own design; previous to this feat, in two months of canoeing, he navigated the length of the Murray River, from its alpine source to the sea. From oars he turned to the new popular sport of motoring and had imported the first De Dion, Cadillac and Oldsmobile cars seen on Victoria's roads. Next was brother Harry, seven years older than Bertram, a Cambridge cox and Boat Club captain for Jesus College; he chose law, won a seat in the Legislative Assembly for two

---

* Constance in May 1906 wed Captain Arthur Fitzpatrick, an aide-de-camp to the governor. The handsome Fitzpatrick soon decamped with an alleged £70,000 dowry. Leila (b. 1875) never wed; it is recorded that family members destroyed her love letters.

** Francis, a fourth brother, died in infancy.

parliaments, and was called to the English bar. *The Times* gave Harry three columns of space, not for a brilliant brief but to report a rather unpleasant judicial separation case brought by his wife who accused him of cruelty while they were on a not-so-happy holiday in Florence.

Finally, at four years older, came Frank (in between, a brother, Francis, had died in childhood) who continued Armytage empire building with 10 stations in Victoria and two in New South Wales. He was a world traveller and collector of many things fine and expensive; in 1888 at Wooloomanata, he cemented Armytage kinship in his marriage to cousin Caroline, a daughter of uncle Felix Ferdinand, of Turkeith, another stronghold in the Western District.

Bertram had to admit that he was the round peg who fitted into none of these brotherly squares. Being commissioned as a justice of the peace, which allowed him to witness other people's statutory declarations and the like, and nothing new for an Armytage, was about the grandest thing that had happened to him since South Africa. He might be saluted for subduing the Boers, but the depressing reality was that he had returned from the war devoid of a career into which he could focus his energies.

The country Bertram had farewelled on Lara platform was not the same on his return. In his absence, Australia had voted for nationhood and with it, in a growing tide of change, the cosy commands of the Victorian Horse Artillery had disappeared. Defence was now a national business, with no particular place for the idle rich. The separate colonial governments, under which he had grown up and where British heritage was the glue of their coexistence, were now linked as states in the glue of Federation. A serious defence department had arisen as a function of the new Commonwealth, absorbing what was worthwhile from the colonial military, and equipping with new style commands of soldiery and seamanship. Gradually it dawned on Bertram that within this structure he might find an escape from an aimless life. Chums in London told him that the War Office was planning an Australian desk as a watchdog on these fledgling warriors who, for instance, demanded their own Australian navy; Cambridge and the Dragoons and the medals might well qualify him for a new career; he must make enquiries. In the meantime, not to tarry. An invitation had arrived to join a deer-stalking party in New Zealand.

Shackleton reached Australia aboard RMS *India* at the end of November 1907, disembarked in Adelaide (having farewelled 'some wealthy Australians who seemed interested in the expedition') and, in response to a public reception, gave a condensed lecture on his plans to reach the South Pole. 'In the very prime of life, about medium height with a well-knit frame, shoulders that denote physical strength, a well poised head, clean shaven face, and an irresistible charm of manner.' On the suburban train journey from Semaphore dock to the city, a reporter from the *Register* introduced his readers to the greatest explorer Adelaide had welcomed since the days of John MacDouall Stuart. With Shackleton cornered in the compartment, the quaint question-and-answer interview began: 'What prompted your expedition?'

> There were several factors. The fact of having been in the Antarctic circle once always makes one want to go again, but the immediate factor was that three other nations were preparing for the same objective – France, Belgium and America. There was no British expedition of any sort contemplated, so I took the matter up and announced, on February 12, that I had sufficient funds to start with. The French Government supported their expedition with £24,000 and it will leave on July 5 next year.
>
> And what equipment will you take?
>
> For this expedition we have 15 strong Manchurian ponies, thoroughly used to the cold; a big team of 12 dogs and a motor car. The car was specially constructed for the purpose. It is a 12–15 b.h.p. New Arrol-Johnston, of a type that has been used

successfully in the deserts of Sudan. It has been fitted with an air-cooled engine, and the exhaust gases are brought around the engine to the carburettor and lubricating parts so as to warm the carburettor before starting. If we get a similar surface to that which we experienced during Captain Scott's dash to the pole, we will do well. Even if the car is able to run only 200 miles, it will relieve the ponies and dogs considerably. The wheels are made of hickory and steel and are 10 inches broad.

What financial support has been given to you by the British Government?

None at all. We did not ask the present government because we knew it was useless. The Geographical Society could not afford support. There are only five or six people who have come forward with financial help. Interest became aroused in England when the King and Queen and the whole Royal Family came on board *Nimrod* at Cowes, and spent about forty minutes on the ship. The interesting thing, of course, was the fact that Her Majesty entrusted me with a Union Jack. This had never been done before to any polar expedition. Queen Alexandra handed me a letter when presenting the flag, in which she wrote:– 'May this Union Jack which I entrust to your keeping, lead you safely to the South Pole'.

In Melbourne on Monday, 2 December Shackleton received a Lord Mayoral welcome, met with the Royal Geographical Society of Victoria, and at eight o'clock in the Freemasons' Hall, Collins Street, with the governor and Lady Talbot attending and 'Tickets Sold Out' on the door, spoke of his 'dash for the Pole' (as the *Age* called it next morning). That night he stayed at the Melbourne Club and one wonders if an Armytage was among the members who shook his hand? After another overnight train journey he faced a repeat performance in Sydney on Friday evening, 5 December, with 4000 clamouring to attend. Next day's *Sydney Morning Herald* reported: 'Possibly the Town Hall has never had a bigger lantern lecture than Lieutenant Shackleton's last night – humorous and enlightening and aiming to stimulate donations to the expedition's appeal over the next few days.' The *Herald* advised its readers that fundraising was the responsibility of two branches of a committee, Sir John Madden's in Victoria and Sir Frederick Darley's in New South Wales; contributions in Sydney should be sent to Mr W. Crummer, Treasurer, Royal Geographical Society, 13 Bridge Street; in Melbourne to Mr T. W. Fowler, Secretary of the Royal Geographical Society, 421 Collins Street.

Donations of £100 each quickly came from the Sydney University Senate, the *Sydney Morning Herald* and *Daily Telegraph*. When the Commonwealth weighed in with £5000, all collected monies were returned to the donors. Despite his need for funds, Shackleton directed that the proceeds from his lectures were to be given to local charities. Money management was never a strong point with The Boss; but it was a gesture that endeared his commanding presence all the more to the Australian populace. It was an exciting time to be in the city. Madam Melba was performing with her Grand Opera Company and Norman Brooks had returned from London with the Davis Cup. But Shackleton had no time to hang around. *Nimrod* had reached New Zealand and his men were waiting.

Among the 400 applicants to join the BAE was Bertram's cousin once or twice removed, Herbert Dyce Murphy. Their relationship went back to the 1860s when George Armytage's daughter, Eliza Anne, married John Rout Hopkins, son of other Western District pioneers. Herbert's mother was a Hopkins, hence the connection that gave him the distinction of being born at Como when his parents, father Alex and mother, a very pregnant Ada Dyce Murphy, came on holiday from their Queensland property, Northampton Downs, which ran 200,000 sheep along the Barcoo. Herbert called Caroline, the chatelaine of Como, his great aunt. His father, a pastoralist and racehorse breeder, was a close friend of Bertram's father, all being prominent members of the Melbourne Club.

It is said that if only half that has been written about Herbert

Dyce Murphy is true, he still led the life of a remarkable and foot-loose adventurer, in some ways like Bertram who was 10 years his senior. He served on Norwegian and Dundee whaling vessels in Arctic waters, and again in the Southern Ocean. But his reputation revolved around quite a different role. With his slim build and fine features, to a point almost effeminate, and dressed in women's clothing he claimed to have served at the turn of the century as a spy for British Military Intelligence, reporting on the railways of northern France and Belgium. Though Herbert offered extensive polar experience Shackleton is said to have politely declined the services of this smooth-featured young man who had spent part of his career dressed as a woman. Never daunted, Herbert exclaimed, 'you need someone to take care of the ponies? I have just the one, my cousin Bertram!' Or so the story goes. As a postscript to his rejection, four years later Herbert went to Antarctica in Douglas Mawson's 1911 Australasian expedition. But he could gain no advice on surviving the ice from his cousin. Bertram by then had been dead for going on two years; Herbert's father, Alex, president of the Melbourne Club, was a pallbearer at the funeral.

CHAPTER 8

THE VOYAGER

Port Lyttelton, snuggled among rolling hills, is the seafarer's door of New Zealand's largest southern city. Christchurch and its port, but half an hour's drive away, are witness to more than a century of Antarctic history as men conclude their business and load their ships for the long voyage south. Scott's first expedition sailed from here in the wooden-walled *Discovery* and almost 10 years later he took an overladen *Terra Nova* on the fateful journey from which some would not return. Byrd, the American, came by with a cargo of flying machines that began a new age of polar exploration.

Within the thick steel plates of a US Navy icebreaker, I was a latter-day traveller to 'the ice' who watched Port Lyttelton's wharves slide peacefully away and just beyond the headland found a wild ocean waiting with its quiver of mighty waves. No one much saw us off, but Shackleton had brass bands, canons firing and a crowd of 30,000 cheering and waving when his British Antarctic Expedition left port on New Year's Day, 1908.

A regatta of gunboats, tugs, ferries and yachts were *Nimrod*'s escorts from the harbour and many an old salt would shake his head at a plimsoll line buried beneath the massive overload of person and provisions. Fifteen Manchurian 'snow ponies' had been brought from a farm in outermost China and freighted via Shanghai and Sydney to the quarantine reserve on Quail Island at Port Lyttelton.

Shortage of space dictated that only 10 of the best could be taken south. These long-haired beasts, secured in wooden pens, were a most treasured cargo; The Boss depended on them to reach the Pole. Nansen had advised him to take dogs rather than ponies but, to his ultimate regret, Shackleton disputed the advice of the great Norwegian ice explorer; anyway, the 12 yelping huskies were soon reduced in number when one drowned beneath a swamping wave.*

In a big wooden crate stood the Arrol Johnston motor car, complete with a range of wheels to let it grip snow and ice. Much was expected of the little machine, made in the factory of James Beardmore, a Scottish industrialist who was the expedition's major backer. Bernard Day, the 24-year-old driver and mechanic, enjoyed telling his doubters that one day machines of its kind might well put the four leggeds out to pasture. Cargo crammed the vessel above deck and below, including Professor David's quarter ton of books and instruments and two 'meteorological kites' designed by the Australian aviation pioneer, Lawrence Hargrave. Food, fuel, medicines, a heap of one-man and three-man sleeping bags, 30 sledges, two crates of Mackinlays whisky, three barrels of beer donated by a New Zealand brewery, a mountain of pony fodder, sewing machines, a printing press, gramophone and kinematographic camera, carbide cylinders for lighting, timbers for the prefabricated hut, and a whaleboat (which Shackleton privately planned to sail back to New Zealand if they were marooned); stores of every kind to sustain an expedition for two years – or how long? Below deck, crew and Shore Party were jammed in quarters ridiculously tight; Oyster Alley was the well chosen name for a boarded-up unventilated section of the hold where the 15 Shore Party tried to sleep which, against sodden bedding and endless crises, wasn't very often.

In the harbour ahead of them waited *Koonya*, a steel-hulled

---

* The dogs were descendants of those used by Carsten Borchgrevink, the Anglo-Norwegian explorer and Australian resident, in the 1898 Southern Cross expedition, based at Cape Adare.

MEMBERS OF THE SHORE PARTY
The British Antarctic Expedition, 1907–1909

Name	Position	Age (1908)
Ernest Henry Shackleton	commander	34
Jameson Boyd Adams	second-in-command, meteorologist	28
Bertram Armytage	general helper, in charge of ponies	39
Sir Philip Lee Brocklehurst	assistant geologist	20
Tannatt William Edgeworth David	director of scientific staff	50
Bernard C. Day	electrician, motor expert	24
Ernest Edward Mills Joyce	in charge of general stores, dogs, sledges,	33
Dr Alistair Forbes Mackay	assistant surgeon	30
Dr Eric Stewart Marshall	surgeon, cartographer	29
George Edward Marston	artist	26
Douglas Mawson	physicist	26
James Murray	biologist	43
Raymond Edward Priestley	geologist	21
William C. Roberts	cook	36
John Robert Francis Wild	in charge of provisions	35

Armytage was the only member of the Shore Party born in Australia: all others members with the exception of Shackleton (Ireland), David (Wales), and Murray (Scotland) were born in England.

steamship engaged courtesy of the New Zealand Government and Union Steamship Company, to tow *Nimrod* to the fringe of the pack ice as a coal saving measure. Within an hour of leaving port, *Nimrod* met an angry ocean head on, plunging and rising on an enormous swell, heeling to 45 degrees in a screaming wind and entering an unrelenting ordeal which would continue unabated for 10 days.* Bertram was granted no time to find his sea legs, soon he was

---

* Shackleton purchased *Nimrod*, an ex-Newfoundland sealer, for £5000. Built at Dundee in 1866 with a hull of oak, greenheart and ironbark the small vessel displaced 334 gross tonnes and measured 136 feet long. Shackleton had the vessel re-rigged from schooner to barquentine and the 60 hp compound steam engine enabled a speed of 6 knots and 8.5 with sail.

struggling to keep the ponies upright as enormous green seas came crashing across the decks and swirled through the scuppers. Alongside him to help protect the ponies in the desperately careering vessel, he had Forbes Mackay, a peppery Scots surgeon who was given the responsibility of 'vet', and Sir Philip Brocklehurst, a 20-year-old Baronet whose mother had given £2000 to the BAE to ease the way for her lordly son's passage; thankfully he also had Frank Wild, a Royal Navy seaman on 'loan' and a veteran of Scott's first expedition.

A veil of unreality must have descended on Bertram as his ship slammed into the high seas of the Southern Ocean, at any moment likely to founder from a water load beyond the capacity of those who struggled to work the undersized pumps. No time for him to consider how one day he was deer hunting in the New Zealand alps and the next inducted into Shackleton's Shore Party, kitting himself on the double in Christchurch and being introduced to a pack of hairy ponies and 14 men, including his fellow countrymen David and Mawson, to bunk and work with at the closest quarters.* Not even much time to think of a wife and a daughter of two years who would receive his farewell by cable. For Blanch it was another abrupt departure of this wandering Armytage male.

In Christchurch purchase had been made of a wardrobe for the ponies. Yellowing pages of the BAE's 'specification of equipment' list 10 horse head collars, 1 carriage whip, 1 twitch, 10 iron picketing pegs, 6 pack saddles 'with Mexican cross pack trees, nummah felt panels, patent hide', plus farrier's pincers, shoeing hammer, rasp, buffer and 2 paring knives.

Fastened in wooden pens, the 10 ponies were tethered athwart ships between the lifeboats – five on the port side, the other five to

---

* Two others aboard *Nimrod*, both 'round trippers', were Edgeworth David's young geology student, Leo Cotton, and George Buckley, a New Zealand sheep farmer who donated £500 to BAE funds.

starboard. By names, from port, they were Socks, Chinaman, Doctor, Orisi, Mac; facing them from starboard were Sandy, Billy, Quan, Zulu, and Nimrod. They were fed a mix of maize and hay contained in individual wooden mangers – until Quan 'the all wise', according to David's voyage notes, discovered that softwood slats made an interesting addition to their diet and soon the rest of the ponies were following suit.

Bertram knew that he was slotted as one of the 'Ors-tralian' afterthoughts, a colonial Johnny-come-lately whose ability to keep safe the expedition's 'legs' would be watched and measured, especially by Mackay who did not hide his hostility toward the colonial clique. On the second day out, the pony Nimrod lost its footing on the heaving deck and fell almost upside down between the slats of the narrow wooden stall. For hours Bertram and his helpers struggled to lift the hapless animal to its feet, but jammed tight within the confines of the stall, all their pulling and levering only added to the stricken animal's distress. By the second day, the only option was to take a revolver and put a bullet through the exhausted animal's skull. Nine ponies left for Bertram's care. Three days later a second pony, Doctor, collapsed from effects of bruising and bleeding in being thrown constantly against the wooden planks. Another bullet through the skull; eight ponies left and not yet across the Antarctic Circle. Fifteen days out from port, *Koonya* dropped the four-inch thick towing hawser and let *Nimrod*, after 1400 battered miles, glide at last into the calmer waters of the Ross Sea pack.

Koonya returned to New Zealand carrying the expedition's mail and Shackleton's report of the voyage which, by prior arrangement, was hurried to the newspapers in Sydney. At Wooloomanata, the family would soon read of Bertram's self-imposed ordeal in choosing Antarctica. Shackleton wrote in the *Sydney Morning Herald*, 5 February 1908:

> Towards afternoon the wind increased greatly, and the *Nimrod* began to ship much water, and to pitch and roll heavily, so much

so that we signalled the *Koonya* at 7 p.m. to go slow till the weather moderated . . . The little *Nimrod* pitched about like a cork on the ocean . . . it needed constant watching to keep the ponies on their feet, for the vessel was rolling 45deg. on either side.

January 3 All the morning a heavy gale and high sea prevented the *Koonya* from towing us more than a knot in the hour, but in the afternoon the weather moderated and we signalled, 'Increase speed'.

January 4 As evening wore on the weather became worse, and we shipped huge quantities of water. So far neither Captain England nor I have had our clothes off, and sleep is a thing we long for. I cannot speak too highly of Captain England's handling of the *Nimrod*. The splendid way in which Captain Evans worked the *Koonya* excited our admiration, and his superb seamanship was a treat to watch.

January 5 Blowing harder than ever. We signalled the *Koonya* to pour oil on the water, so that we astern might get the benefit. It certainly has been of assistance to us.

January 6 The weather was better towards noon, and we went ahead full speed. A huge sea 40ft high, is now running abeam. Captain England and myself have slept hardly at all yet.

January 7 Our worst day so far. A mountainous sea and a whole gale. The squalls were of hurricane force. Sprays go over the fore-yard, and the *Koonya* disappears from view every few minutes, because of the intervening mountain seas. The wind simply shrieks through the rigging. We are using oil all the time.

January 8 A heavy gale and terrific squalls with a high sea. Heavy seas stove in part of the bulwarks forward.

January 9 This morning we had a moderate wind, with a high, confused sea and were able to go full speed. In the afternoon the wind again increased, the squalls being of hurricane force, and the sea very high. More of the bulwarks were washed away.

January 10 Continuous rain, and wind moderating, is the story of to-day. Most of us have managed to wash the salt from our faces. We were getting pickled during the last week.

January 11 Same old game again! Strong increasing wind and rising sea, which increased so much that we had to keep away. In the afternoon this particular specimen of sea was a dangerous one, and gave us some anxiety.

January 12 A high sea was running early in the morning, which gradually moderated, and at 4 p.m. we were able to steer south again.

January 13 Wonder of wonders! A gentle breeze from the eastward. The ship looks like a drying green on a Monday morning, as blankets, coats, boots, etc., are all recovering from a thorough salt-water soaking. Keeping a sharp look-out for ice, which we may see any time.

January 14 Fine clear day. Passed two icebergs this morning. The weather is rapidly growing colder. We ought to see the pack any time.

January 15 Sighted the pack at 9 a.m. Misty weather. Am now going to let go the *Koonya*.

CHAPTER 9

REACHING McMURDO

My Antarctic curtain-raiser was the steaming crater of a snow-clad volcano; all the more memorable when seen through the idling propeller of a limping Air Force transport. Below lay Ross Island on McMurdo Sound, the place of Scott and Shackleton, crowned mightily by the white dome of Mount Erebus. An iceberg-littered sea, across which little ships must sail, stretched away to the north; to the south the Transantarctic Mountains, peak after glistening peak which explorers must climb, marching toward the Pole. Bertram Armytage and I shared this awesome introduction to Antarctica; or so I like to think. Mine from the silver belly of a C124 Globemaster at the end of a 10-hour night flight from Christchurch, New Zealand; his of 50 years before, at sea level from the deck of a battered wooden vessel that had been 14 days sailing from New Zealand.

Almost a week had been wasted since *Nimrod* broke through the Ross Sea pack in a futile search for Shackleton's choice of a landing place on King Edward VII Land, at the far eastern end of the Great Ice Barrier. Hummocky ice and grounded 'bergs barred the coast and to push further east risked *Nimrod*'s timbers and Captain Rupert England was having none of that. They turned toward an indentation at the eastern end of the Barrier where Shackleton had landed with Scott making the first balloon ascent of the ice in 1902; Antarctica's first aeronauts, Scott described them. Bertram was nominated to accompany The Boss and two others to lay advance depots across the Barrier for next summer's march to the Pole. But fracturing ice thwarted their plans and Bertram lost his chance of a baptismal journey into unknown Antarctica. In fact, Shackleton established that where *Nimrod* moored was 10 miles south of his 1902 position, such was the magnitude of the break-out; the risk of finding their camp adrift on an iceberg was not to be contemplated and the hunt for a base site resumed.

Progress seemed agonisingly slow through the last week of January as Captain England gingerly surveyed the 400 miles of the Barrier's towering cliffs on a westwards course that must take the party ultimately to the known haven of Ross Island on McMurdo Sound, first discovered by Captain James Clark Ross RN in 1841. Under sail to conserve fuel, the overloaded ship in its wallowing and rolling began to blunt the optimism of a Shore Party dismayed at seeing their bruised ponies in worsening condition and increasingly anxious to be ashore. This feeling of adversity was not helped when a swinging derrick hook struck Aeneas Mackintosh in the face, leaving his right eye a black and bloodied hole. Under a compress of chloroform he lay on the saloon floor as surgeons Marshall, Mackay and Michell, the ship's doctor, using improvised instruments, removed the damaged eye and with it Mackintosh's hope of being part of Shackleton's expedition. (Six years later he got a second chance to serve with Shackleton; at Cape Evans a plaque bearing his name looks across the ice of McMurdo Sound where he and a companion in a reckless attempt at crossing were last seen.) Finally the much-boasted merits of the Arrol Johnston car were in doubt when, landed on the ice for a test run, it did nothing more than dig a hole in the snow with its spinning wheels. Perhaps all this drama was just so much background blur for Bertram. His responsibility to Shackleton lay in the eight ponies locked on *Nimrod*'s deck and in making sure that no less than eight ponies safely reached wherever they would land.

At the start of February they sailed into McMurdo Sound where, as was generally known, Shackleton had promised (or, rather, was it that he had been pressured by antagonists in the Royal Geographical Society into giving such an undertaking?) that he would not base an expedition on Ross Island which Captain Scott regarded as 'his' territory for a future expedition. To his men gathered in the wardroom Shackleton admitted that it was a matter of 'damned if I do, and damned if I don't'. He had done his best at King Edward VII Land. But in no way would he submit to a mindless code of 'play the game, old man' that belonged to a departed Victorian society. 'I know in my heart I am right,' he said. 'We have to secure a solid rock foundation for our winter home.' With 2400 cases of stores to unload, there was no time to waste. All agreed with him except, perhaps, for Marshall, the argumentative and self-righteous doctor and cartographer who did not appear to find much agreeable in any of Shackleton's decisions.

On 1 February, while searching for a landing place, Bertram was one of a five-man team led by Professor David that made for 'nearby' Tent Island. Antarctica gave them a whisper of its trickery when the island proved much more distant than their estimate, an unsuspected gulf of open water thwarted their attempt to reach its shore, and on the hurried return with a blizzard threatening, two members fell through thin sea ice and had to be rescued.

The ice-jammed southern reaches of McMurdo Sound ruled that at least Shackleton would not land at Hut Point where *Discovery* had anchored in 1901 and a place particularly sacred to the demanding Scott, though it offered a preferable location. In a decision he made on 3 February, the party would settle for Cape Royds, named after the Discovery's first lieutenant, which lay some 23 miles to the north of Hut Point – in effect a further 23 miles to reach the Pole. Ironically, seeing how he opposed Shackleton's occupation of Ross Island, it was Scott who, with Wilson, first camped at Cape Royds in January 1904, discovering the Adelie penguins and in his journal recording 'words fail me to describe what a delightful and interesting spot this is'. The site where they could build a hut at 77°31'S. lay in a small depression between the prominence of the Cape and a rocky ridge which, it was hoped, would blunt the worst of the winds. The small freshwater Pony Lake, as they knew it, lay across from the site and beyond it was the guano-carpeted penguin rookery, in summer the source of incessant chatter and unpleasant smells.* Bertram might have viewed with diffidence his meeting with an Adelie population which offered no real sport. Yet of the birds they would soon slaughter, David recorded:

> They are the dearest, quaintest and most winsome birds imaginable. They came toddling along like a lot of babies who have just learned to walk, balancing themselves upright, their little pink legs and webbed feet twinkling between their snow-white feathers and the level carpet of snow over which they were travelling. Every now and then they waved their flippers to us, as though to signal to us to wait for them. In a minute or so they had reached us, and came within a foot or two of us, and discussed our appearance with one another quite unreservedly.

The nightmare of finding a site to land was about to be replaced by another. In the turmoil of crossing the Southern Ocean, the crew and expeditioners, personified in Shackleton and *Nimrod*'s master Rupert England, were united in the single purpose of keeping their ship afloat. Upon reaching McMurdo, the theme of survival changed. With 180 tons of cargo to be unloaded, The Boss and his fellow expeditionaries were intent on getting ashore as quickly as possible with a minimum of wasted effort. But on the water the captain controlled their destiny and this master's prime concern

---

* It was later established that this was the most southerly Adelie rookery in Antarctica.

lay in protecting his ship from damage and disaster, even if it meant losing precious hours, maybe days, standing offshore and dodging drifting ice. England's caution was soon seen as excessive and of unforgivable timidity. Three days had passed since Shackleton had given the order to unload, yet England's response seemed as nothing less than total disregard for the Shore Party's needs. Keeping *Nimrod* out in the Sound at the edge of the fast ice condemned these 15 men into demon-driven shifts of lifting, lugging and dragging across a mile and more of hazardous ice when, they reckoned, with a little more courage, the Captain could have taken them within 100 yards of their chosen landing spot beneath the headland of Cape Royds, which they named Back Door Bay.

Against the spectre of a frozen Sound, no delay was possible in the 24 hours of polar daylight. After the precious motor car was hurried ashore, their next most precious cargo was the ponies, lowered in their pens, one by one, from the ship and urged as fast as stiff and weakened limbs would allow across the ice and up the steep slope of Cape Royds, to be tethered against a rocky ridge near the site of their hut. Appearing oblivious to past weeks of torment, the beasts were soon pawing the snow as if at home in their native Manchuria and licking thirstily at the ice crust, which Bertram and fellow members of their self-styled 'Cavalry Club' welcomed with misplaced relief. Despite the bruised and restive condition, they submitted to a harness and began drawing laden sledges across the ice from ship to shore.

The survival of Bertram's ponies was abruptly put at risk when a hissing fissure opened across the sea ice. Bertram, commanding the first sledge, managed to jump his pony across the gap before the animal had a chance to hesitate. Forbes Mackay, leading a second pony (Chinaman) had no such luck. Confronted by a widening split beneath his hoofs, the animal reared backwards, stumbled and fell into the icy waters, destined for mincemeat in a pincer movement of the floe, or be taken by the jaws of a lurking killer whale. Somehow neither disaster happened and after two hours of pulling and levering, Mackay and others who had run from the ship finally managed by sheer brute force to bring the frantic beast back on the ice where half a flask of brandy was emptied down his throat to stem the spasms of violent shivering.

Shackleton ruled an end to pony journeys from the ship, which meant more agony of man-hauling for him and his men. In his diary, Shackleton reviewed it as 'the most uncomfortable fortnight of my life' – which signalled all the elements were in place for whatever new crisis was ready to ambush them. This moment came without warning when the hard-ice edge beneath Cape Royds suddenly began to disintegrate, threatening to dump their accumulated stores into the depths of the Bay. All hands were summoned to form a human chain to drag the heaps of crates and boxes, timbers and barrels to the safety of rocky ground; simultaneously *Nimrod* was signalled to come close in to avoid any further risky unloading. It was about this time – probably late on 17 February, no one was ever sure exactly when and Bertram left no record – that the test of wills between The Boss and the master of his ship reached breaking point.

England, fearful of the drifting floes, began backing *Nimrod* away from the ice edge. An exasperated Shackleton raced to the bridge, grabbed the engine room telegraph and pushed it across to Ahead; an outraged captain slammed his hand atop Shackleton's and dragged the telegraph back to Astern. For a moment the two figures of authority in conflict faced each other, glowering, speechless, while Bertram and the others looked on in silence. In the privacy of the captain's cabin, England refused Shackleton's suggestion that, on grounds of ill health and nervous exhaustion, he should surrender command to J. K. Davis, the lanky, red-headed first officer. A compromise allowed *Nimrod* to be moored in an agreed accessible position against an outermost floe, letting Shackleton and his men resume the final task of unloading coal supplies, without which the one-room hut at Cape Royds would turn into an icy tomb.

Despite the truce, England had given little ground and to reach a new landing point at Back Door Bay they had to take the whale-boat, stacked with almost a ton of coal in 20 canvas sacks, on a hazardous course across a half mile of open sea until they entered the pack. With Davis steering, oars and gloved fists pushed and prodded the ice aside to reach the shore where companions waited with ponies attached to sledges for the climb to the fuel dump beside the hut. For 12 hours without a pause, they lowered the heavy sacks from the ship's deck and pulled across the sea to moor against an unfriendly ice foot that reared some 12 feet above them. Bertram was one of the crew and like the others in the boat – David, Mawson, Michell and Davis – he soon became unrecognisable beneath a grimy coating of coal dust. But conspicuous strength at the oars and obvious muscular energy soon identified the Australian as someone in whom The Boss could place his trust. In a letter to his wife, Emily, sent with the ship, Shackleton wrote of 'a splendid man, obedient, reliable, ready for any work . . . gets on with all, extremely popular because he is a man of the world and knows the ways of younger men. He [Armytage] was the 1st to make the English section reconsider their attitude to Australians'.*

Yet the desperate unloading routine won no reprieve from the blizzard of 18 February from the south-east that whipped McMurdo Sound with demoniac force for three relentless days. Shackleton and half his Shore Party, Bertram included, were stranded and help-less aboard the ship in a wind reaching 100 miles an hour; all visibility was lost and to turn the helm was like battling with concrete. Despite engines churning full ahead, *Nimrod* was forced some 50 miles north of Cape Royds amid ghostly drifting 'bergs and grinding floes, in a 20-degree drop in temperature that encrusted decks and masts with a lather of ice that threatened the very stability of the vessel.

---

* Marshall referred to the arrival of David and Mawson as 'Jonahs we could do without'. The fourth Australian, David's student Leo Cotton, left aboard *Nimrod* to return to Australia as planned.

Ashore, around a half-completed hut* and trembling against the onslaught of the gale, the remainder of the Shore Party crouched in makeshift shelters, wondering if they would ever see The Boss again and watching sheets of wind-driven sea smother the camp site and its jumble of crated stores beneath an icy blanket that, allowing they survived, would take weeks, if ever, to locate and dig free.

When the wind dropped on 21 February and the last of the barely adequate 18 tons of coal was ready to row ashore, Captain England waited not one more minute. Shackleton and his crew scrambled down the ladder to push off with laden boat, while 'Full ahead' rang from the bridge. Free of entrapment in McMurdo Sound, on 22 February *Nimrod* steered north for New Zealand and the calm and order of civilisation. In the captain's locker, among all the Shore Party's farewell mail, in a letter marked 'confidential' and addressed to Joseph Kinsey, his Christchurch attorney, Shackleton asked for Rupert England's resignation as *Nimrod*'s skipper.

Among coal-blackened figures, Bertram stood on the promontory of Cape Royds watching the little ship sail toward the open waters of the Ross Sea, answering the three cheers of the departing crew with the throaty response of 15 exhausted men; knowing from henceforth they were cut off from the rest of the world and mostly ignorant of the angry ice continent on which they dared to settle. However the oncoming winter left little time for personal emotions. *Nimrod* was scarcely out of sight when Shackleton summoned Bertram and others to kill 100 penguins as emergency provisions.

Meanwhile, the chaps back at the Club, not to mention the folk around Werribee and Wooloomanata, would be a trifle concerned about their wandering boy when in the daily press of mid April they saw the headline 'Leaders Reported Dissension – Captain England Goes Home'. The story originated with H. B. Bull, a crew member

---

* The hut was assembled in 10 days by a five-man Shore Party under leadership of Harry Dunlop, the ship's chief engineer. However another month elapsed before it was fully fitted out and weatherproof.

A penguin rookery was useful to us. The birds were there when we first arrived. We went in amongst them and killed about a hundred of them. We did not shoot them. It was mere slaughter. They had absolutely no fear of men. They did not know what man was, and let us walk right in among them and knock them over. Even after we had killed as many they still betrayed no fear. We did not pluck or dress the birds. We just flung them on the roof of the hut. There they became frozen hard – a natural refrigerating chamber. When we wanted to use one, we went to the larder on the roof, took the bird inside, thawed it out and prepared it for cooking. They made very good eating indeed, and were a welcome addition to our provisions. We also drew largely on the penguin rookery for eggs. The eggs are very large with small yolks and large whites. They were very nice to eat.

[Bertram Armytage interview, Sydney, 6 April 1909]

of *Nimrod* who had 'just arrived in Melbourne on furlough'. Mr Bull said he was at the helm when the clash occurred between Shackleton and the captain.

> The *Nimrod* was in 13 fathoms. 'Please go further in,' said Lieutenant Shackleton. 'It is impossible,' said Captain England. After some argument, the lieutenant made towards the telegraph as if intending to signal 'full speed ahead', but the captain got in ahead of him and said, 'I am master of this ship. It is not possible to take her nearer land with safety.' Then they had some more talk and went below.

Referring to the news of England's resignation he continued:

> We got in on Sunday or Monday night. He called the men again and said, 'I have to say goodbye. The unexpected has happened since I saw you last' and he did not say much more, for his

feelings got too much for him. I could see he was nigh crying. We men were very much troubled about this, and when we got forward several said they'd leave with the captain . . .*

Probably much of this drama had passed over Bertram's head, for the ponies were his concern.

---

* *Sydney Morning Herald*, 13 April 1908.

CHAPTER 10

VOLCANO

Before winter and darkness came, Shackleton decided they should accept the challenge of Mount Erebus, the active volcano which trailed a feathery cloud across the heavens behind Cape Royds. Reaching the volcano's summit, Shackleton stated, would be 'an exercise of pleasurable excitement' for the young expedition, as well as launching into 'their serious scientific program of geology and meteorology'.

Shackleton selected a three-man climbing party comprising Edgeworth David (always 'the Prof'), Mawson and Mackay. Three others, Adams, Marshall and Brocklehurst, were enrolled in a support party, with instructions they could also attempt the summit if it did not impede the climbers. The six set out after an early breakfast on 5 March, equipped with ice axes, improvised crampons and dragging an 11-foot sledge laden with provisions and camping gear sufficient, if need be, for 10 days.

Bertram was among the rest of the expedition who marched beside the Erebus men, helping to drag their 600 lb sledge across the snow-topped rocky ridges beyond the hut. The Boss took photographs and they all cheered as the figures dissolved into the snowfield at the base of the great white mountain.

Armed with the powerful deer stalking telescope that he had brought from New Zealand, Bertram's responsibility – and a welcome distraction from the ponies – was watching for the climbers' progress as they ascended the mountain. On their third day out, he reported sighting six tiny dots moving slowly one after the other against a background of snow; this gave Shackleton the understanding that Adams' men were still with the climbers and that all six were roped together, meaning the sledge had been dropped. Next day Bertram reported that rolling storm clouds had obliterated the upper slopes of Erebus and nothing could be seen. Not until later would they learn that within that cloud, in minus 20 degrees temperature, all six were battling against a shrieking blizzard that threatened to blow them from their tent into a mist-filled void. For 32 hours they were imprisoned in their three-man sleeping bags, only a nibble of chocolate and a plasmon biscuit for nourishment, and nothing to drink. Brocklehurst declared it wasn't much of a way to celebrate his 21st birthday. Climbing resumed on 9 March above an elevation of 9000 feet in a minus 30 degree chill and thinning air. Mackay fainted from exertion in trying to hack his way up a snow precipice, while Brocklehurst hobbled to a standstill knowing that within the heavy ski boots, all feeling in his toes seemed to be lost. In pausing briefly to cook and camp above the clouds, they were rewarded at dawn with the incredible vision of Erebus projected by the rising sun in complete silhouette from above McMurdo Sound to the Western Mountains. But with the summit in sight and desperate to escape another night on the volcano, they could not delay. Bertram captured them again on his telescope, the same six black dots moving along the skyline towards the crater, and then they were lost.

On the morning of their sixth day out, Shackleton was working outside the hut when he saw a group of men stumbling toward him from the direction of Blue Lake. 'Did you climb it?' he shouted. Then again. In reply, one waved his arms above his head. Within the shelter of the hut, champagne 'which tasted like nectar' was served all around as the climbers forged into a mighty breakfast of porridge, bread, ham and honey. Bertram put away his telescope and joined a hushed audience that listened to the Prof's story of valuable finds of pumice stone, sulphur and felspar crystals. And how at about 10 am on 10 March, breathing with difficulty in the sulphurous air, they made their way through an outlandish icy garden of green and white frozen fumarole sculptures, and across a pavement of sparkling felspar crystals, to reach 'the verge of a vast abyss'. Above them ascended a 1000-foot swaying white column of steam while from below issued a continuous hissing, punctuated from within the volcano's bowels by a dull booming sound which, with the smell of burning sulphur, brought huge globular masses of vapour rushing upward. Mawson, at some risk to his life, scrambled around the rim to photograph them standing on the edge of a crater estimated to be 900 feet deep and measuring half a mile across; from aneroid and hypsometer readings, they determined the height of Erebus at 13,370 feet; in short they had conquered Antarctica's highest then known mountain.*

As a postscript to the laborious climb, and to escape threatening blizzards, they bundled up their gear and provisions and, on reaching the start of a long, steep slope, pushed them over the side. Then they followed themselves, using their ice axes for brakes as they glissaded in a series of helter-skelter rushes through the crisp snow, descending 5000 feet in a matter of four hours.

When the bad weather relented, Bertram went out with Adams, Wild, Joyce and the irrepressible David to retrieve the 11-foot sledge loaded with pumice and felspar specimens which the exhausted climbers had found too heavy to drag home. The ascent of Mount Erebus came at some cost. On 5 April, Marshall amputated a withered big toe from Brocklehurst's right foot which, like Mackintosh's lost eye, ended the young aristocrat's hope of joining the Pole party.

---

* Elevation of Mount Erebus has since been determined at 12,450 feet (3795 metres). The Vinson Massif in the Sentinel Range of Western Antarctica is the highest known peak at 16,070 feet (4897 metres).

Bertram's major task lay along the wall on the lee side of the hut where the ponies were tethered in their tarpaulin-roofed stalls, walled in by cases of provisions and feed. Early each day he gave them a quota of maize and fodder, with the supplement of a syrupy honey mixture known as the Maujee ration which they all lapped up. He combed their coats, checked their hooves and, one at a time if weather permitted, led them on a little circular trot around the patch of flat snow, barely a stone's throw away, which they named 'Green Park'. A chain was then fastened to contain them within the stalls, for no leather halter would survive their constant gnawing (which had happened when Grisi escaped, the alarm only being raised by the barking dogs) and the prospect of a pony running loose into the blizzardly darkness was one of the unthinkables.

Fridtjof Nansen had advised them to take dogs and not put over-much faith in ponies. But Shackleton remembered the dogs' disappointing performance on the Discovery expedition and, instead, voted for hoofs rather than paws, taking the 15 ponies at the outset and just 10 dogs. Like the Arrol Johnston motor car, the ponies were the first of their kind to go south. Long haired and squat, yet cunning and intelligent, the Manchurian breed was a world apart from the haughty blue bloods of the cavalry and the gallant chestnuts of Werribee Park's half battery. But the snow breeding of Manchuria equipped them for a task no horse, no matter how well bred, could tolerate. The argument against dogs proposed that a single pony would do the work of at least 10 dogs; in icy temperatures, it had the strength to march 20 or 30 miles a day, hauling a 1200 lb sledge. Further, at camping they was just one animal to care for, not packs of 10, and if they had to be put down because of injury, a single pony represented a lot more meat than a dog.

No matter how sadly they compared in shape with the Western District's graceful steeds, Bertram knew he was their number one carer, and to prime them for the Pole was the name of the game. The eight ponies that came ashore at Cape Royds had rapidly acclimatised themselves to Antarctic living. Everyone remarked how, once free of the ship and on solid ground, they were prancing and rolling in the snow of the sandy beach, and licking enthusiastically at the ice.

Zulu was the first to die, on the eve of the Erebus party's departure. Marshall's post mortem revealed a stomach heavy with a mixture of sand and felspar crystals. After another short, inexplicable illness, Sandy died next day and when Joyce and Day cut him open, the pony's gut disclosed another load, equal to about 14 lbs, of the same volcanic sand and crystals. A week later, Billy fell to his knees, rolled over and expired from the corrosive poisoning of eating impregnated wood shavings that had been packed around the scientists' flasks and chemicals. On 14 March, Mac collapsed from the deadly volcanic diet; he was shot to end his misery.

Lack of salt was to blame. Shackleton had voiced his concern that the ponies' diet might be short of salt, though Bertram disagreed. They were tethered where sea water blown ashore in the big storm of 3 February formed an icy crust mixed with the sand and felspar. In their thirst for salt, they had devoured the ground beneath their feet and filled their stomachs with a fatal load.

Shackleton said he needed a minimum of six ponies for the expedition's marches; now they were four. In less than two weeks they had lost four irreplaceable animals. For a start it meant that the South Magnetic Pole party would be condemned to man-hauling. Bertram reflected how he had watched and grinned as his charges nibbled at the ice, not understanding the danger. He had taken no precautions to restrain Mac from gnawing into the fatal sawdust. His companions, including The Boss himself, said they all shared a common ignorance and no individual was to blame. But who was the minder? Who was supposed to be the horsey bloke, the Australian bushman, the cavalryman from the 6th Dragoons? This is why he had been enlisted. And he had let them down.

Shackleton, in a stern change of attitude, is reported telling Bertram to take a hold of himself; in latter-day language, to 'snap out of it': to rid himself of the depression which swirled over him like a black cloud, and did neither himself nor his companions any favours. How was it, he was asked, that 14 men packed in the tight confines of the hut through winter darkness could get along together, and yet one other could not? Priestly observed Bertram's spasms of dark introspection. Brocklehurst was an unforgiving critic. Others spoke of haunted eyes that betrayed a darkened soul, and wondered at the scars he carried from the war. Yet this was the wealthy chap, the supposed good mixer who was known in Melbourne's clubs and those of London, the champion rower who had been at Cambridge.

The truth is that Bertram in lapsing back into despondency quickly portrayed himself as the isolated one, an older man who had not much in common with the rest; an outsider, one who had no profession or trade, unlike Priestly or Murray or Mawson, or Day and Marston. The ponies were his reason for being at Cape Royds and only Quan, Socks, Grisi and Chinaman remained. Though his task was still to feed and groom them, others were now involved. The Boss said he wanted the ponies to recognise those who might lead in the summer marches and they were not to be ridden – which only served to prove he was even more superfluous. Not helping Bertram's condition were some of his noted eccentricities. Marshall told of his habit of punctuating his conversation with exclamations of 'What!What!' which earned him a derisive nick-name. Shackleton would refer to him as ever cheerful, obliging and helpful; but those remarks had to await an obituary.

The hut at Cape Royds had never looked so neat. The tumble of blizzard-scattered boxes and crates had been stacked against the wall, the kennels put upright, the pony stalls cleaned out; all as Shackleton and his men wanted it as the winter of '08 descended. Acclimatised or not to the wafting odour of guano from the nearby Adelie rookery, Bertram began a vigorous daily exercise program, calculating that a sprint six times up and down their 'Green Park' equalled a mile. Depending on those wayward moods, he might be inclined while daylight and weather allowed to join in the football or hockey played on a snow-flecked surface of rocky kenyite lava. Just a half mile to the north lie a series of frozen freshwater lakes, another discovery of the Shackleton expedition. Nearest and largest is the intensely vivid Blue Lake, the centre of BAE 'snow sports' where tobogganing down a 200-foot slope, as Bertram did with Bernard Day, shot them torpedo-like across a glassy speedway. The same slopes witnessed David's sole attempt to fly his Hargrave box kite, alas no match for an Antarctic gale, and Eric Marshall's furious hand-cranking of the Kinematograph camera. Before winter closed in, all these outlets for cooped-up energies were made to shouts and laughter, only dampened by the sudden advance of a blizzard which could freeze the unguarded man.

In his other role of 'general duties', Bertram's muscular talents were summoned to assist the expedition's scientist team who, in the Prof's words, found Cape Royds 'a veritable treasure house'. David and Priestly tapped enthusiastically among the hundreds of erratic boulders that lay scattered towards the slopes of Mount Erebus. Adams, the meteorologist, tended his instruments and chronometers, and contemplated a monstrous weather vane in the vapour cloud issuing from the volcano's summit. To Mawson it was 'a new kind of laboratory' and the geologist-turned-physicist measured atmospheric electricity, in darkness observed the aurora and immersed himself in the intricacy of the ice structures surrounding the Cape. As evidence of everyone lending a hand with collecting, in the report of the BAE's scientific investigations, James Murray wrote 'Armytage found a sea-urchin during a walk on the sea-ice . . . and while [we were] landing he picked up the first scrap of sea-weed'. For Murray, the imperturbable Scots biologist, delight lay in finding the teeming microscopic life of the rotifer that flourished through thaw and freeze beneath the crust of the freshwater lakes. With a rope lowered through the ice cracks, one of Bertram's jobs was to haul Murray's makeshift marine dredge along the Bay floor and, in checking for algae growth and temperature, to lower himself into the 15-foot shaft they had cut through the Blue Lake's frozen crust; once he had to make a desperate escape when disturbed water gushed up the shaft, threatening to engulf him.

The backdrop to their labours and ramblings lay in the incomparable view across McMurdo Sound to the Western Mountains where, in the Prof's words, the south polar sun made 'tints of greenish-purple, blue and amethyst on peaks rising above grand glacier-cut valleys, and golden light reflected on the surface of the great glacier'. It gave the feeling, he said, 'that one was seeing something in the way of world beauty never seen anywhere else and one longed to be able to convey the glory of it to those who dwell equator-wards of the Antarctic Circle'. And in Shackleton's eyes, 'the sunsets are poems'.

The scene that greeted Bertram and his comrades has not changed, still startling in the sheer icy beauty of those peaks and glaciers pastel painted across a far horizon. When the door of the old hut opens you feel like asking: 'Where is everyone?' Certain visitors have reported the eerie sensation of hearing men's distant voices. Edward VII and his Queen still stare regally from the wall; tins of Coleman's mustard, Rowntree's cocoa, Lipton tea and Bird's egg custard are stacked neatly on the shelves; next to them, bottled pickles, Sunlight soap, tins of curried rabbit and legs of ham still in the original cloths. Shackleton had the name of looking after his men and in the larder did not deny them. Mrs Sam's slow-combustion stove that ate a quarter ton of anthracite coal each week and sustained life at around 16 degrees or a little more through the chilly months of winter darkness is ready for the match to turn cold iron into a sizzling hotplate for chef Roberts' porridge and roast penguin breast or slabs of New Zealand mutton, or maybe thick steaks of the Weddell seal that, out on the sea ice, had meekly accepted the slaughterman's club.

To the right of the hut's inner end is where Bertram shared a little cubicle, about six feet wide and seven feet deep, with young baronet Brocklehurst, an Eton and Cambridge (but Trinity College) man

Top: The towing steamer, *Koonya,* as seen from *Nimrod* among the green rollers of the Southern Ocean. The stormy 10-day tow covered 1400 miles (2240 km).
NATIONAL LIBRARY OF AUSTRALIA

Above: The BAE artist, George Marston, depicts a wild moment in crossing the Southern Ocean where two ponies perished. NATIONAL LIBRARY OF AUSTRALIA

Below: Chart. Cape Royds and surrounds where the expedition came ashore. FROM SHACKLETON'S *HEART OF THE ANTARCTIC*

Right: Hazards of crumbling ice, blizzard and rising seas faced the expedition in their non-stop effort to land 2400 packing cases at Cape Royds before the ship was forced to sail. A. W. ALLEN PHOTO ALBUMS, STATE LIBRARY OF NSW

Below right: Nimrod, a 300-ton Dundee-built former sealer, moored near a tabular 'berg in the Ross Sea. A. W. ALLEN PHOTO ALBUMS, STATE LIBRARY OF NSW

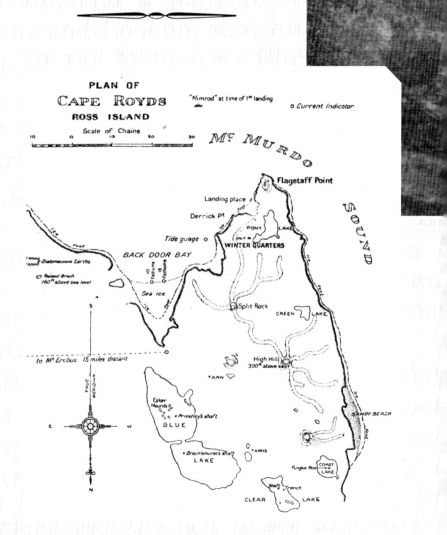

PLAN OF

CAPE ROYDS

ROSS ISLAND

Scale of Chains

"Nimrod" at time of 1st landing

o *Current Indicator*

Mᶜ MURDO

SOUND

Flagstaff Point

Landing place

Derrick Pt

Tide guage o

PONY LAKE

WINTER QUARTERS

BACK DOOR BAY

TARN
TARN Diatomaceous Earths

o Raised Beach
160ᶠᵗ above sea level

Sea ice

Split Rock

GREEN LAKE

to Mᵗ Erebus. 15 miles distant

High Hill
300ᶠᵗ above sea

TARN

TRUE MERIDIAN

Esker
Mounds
• Priestley's shaft

BLUE

LAKE

• Brocklehurst's shaft

TARNS

SANDY BEACH

Fungus Pool

COAST
LAKE

Shell Trench

CLEAR LAKE

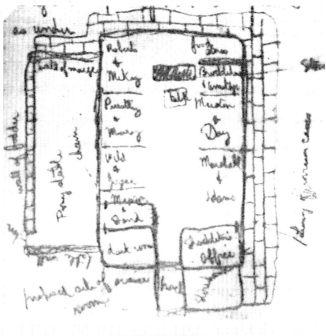

Top: Members of the 15-man Shore Party assembled at Cape Royds; 400 men applied to join Shackleton's expedition. Bertram is in the second row, far right.

Above: Raymond Priestley's sketch of the interior layout of the winter quarters hut at Cape Royds. 'Brocklehurst and Armytage' are near the top right corner.

Top: For protection, Shackleton's men built the winter quarters hut amid the volcanic scoria of a low rocky hill, and found their noisy and smelly summer neighbours to be Antarctica's most southerly Adelie penguin rookery. COLIN MONTEATH PHOTOGRAPH

Above: A priceless relic of Antarctica's heroic age, the hut at Cape Royds is now visited by tourists but protected under strict conservation rules. CATHERINE BURKE

Top left: Bertram Armytage regards a Weddell seal that may soon fall victim to his club. 'There is no sport here,' he remarked. Earlier he had helped in gathering a food supply of 100 Adelie penguins. A. W. ALLEN PHOTO ALBUMS, STATE LIBRARY OF NSW

Left: A seal-hunting party wanders the sea ice in search of meat for the winter supply. A. W. ALLEN PHOTO ALBUMS, STATE LIBRARY OF NSW

Above: Bertram stands among ice flowers on fresh sea-ice growth as winter temperatures approach. Behind him is the accumulated lava from **Mt Erebus.** NATIONAL LIBRARY OF AUSTRALIA

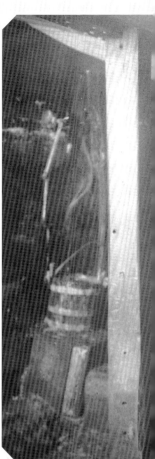

Top left: Eight ponies were in Bertram Armytage's care when the expedition reached Cape Royds. For daily exercise he led them at a trot around the frozen ground. NATIONAL LIBRARY OF AUSTRALIA

Left: Bertram's sledge, now in the collection of Museum Victoria, is constructed of ash on a hickory frame, with the platform fashioned from Vanesta packing-case timbers marked 'dried eggs'. MUSEUM VICTORIA

Above: Each morning at 7.30, Bertram's task was to feed his charges their first meal of the day in a chilly enclosure rigged alongside the winter quarters hut. A. W. ALLEN PHOTO ALBUMS, STATE LIBRARY OF NSW

Top left: George Marston, the BAE artist, drew this impression of his team mates reaching the crest of Mt Erebus. *AURORA AUSTRALIS*, NATIONAL LIBRARY OF AUSTRALIA

Top right: Douglas Mawson, from the University of Adelaide, was in the six-man party that conquered Mt Erebus. His role in the BAE would lead to a famous career in polar science and exploration. NATIONAL LIBRARY OF AUSTRALIA

Above: Fifteen miles (24 km) from Cape Royds lay the icy slopes of Antarctica's active volcano, 12,458 ft (3795 m) Mt Erebus. A. W. ALLEN PHOTO ALBUMS, STATE LIBRARY OF NSW

The BAE party stands at the edge of the 900 ft deep crater of Mt Erebus in early March, 1908. Reaching the 12,458 ft (3795 m) crater of the active volcano was the expedition's first major feat; the leader was the Australian scientist, Professor Edgeworth David, and the photograph is Mawson's. NATIONAL LIBRARY OF AUSTRALIA

Above: Ponies transporting bagged coal on sledges at Back Door Bay. In all, 18 tons of coal had to be unloaded for the hut's supply. A. W. ALLEN PHOTO ALBUMS, STATE LIBRARY OF NSW

Right: Exercising the ponies on the beach at Cape Royds: for some it would bring a fatal result. A. W. ALLEN PHOTO ALBUMS, STATE LIBRARY OF NSW

Above right: On rocky ground behind Cape Royds, Bertram (right) assists a young geologist, Raymond Priestly, in seeking volcanic specimens for the BAE's collection. NATIONAL LIBRARY OF AUSTRALIA

Detail from image at right.

Above: Aurora Australis, the first book published in Antarctica, printed at the hut during the winter of 1908. NATIONAL LIBRARY OF AUSTRALIA

Right: Despite a darkened world around them, expedition members brighten their mid winter with the traditional Antarctic feast held amid the close confines of the hut; a smiling Bertram Armytage sits at the bottom left-hand corner of the table. A. W. ALLEN PHOTO ALBUMS, STATE LIBRARY OF NSW

Above right: Frank Wild is absorbed in sledge repairs watched by other expedition members, including Bertram Armytage, standing in the background. An advertisement for 'Ladies Corsets' is fixed to the far wall. NATIONAL LIBRARY OF AUSTRALIA

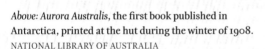

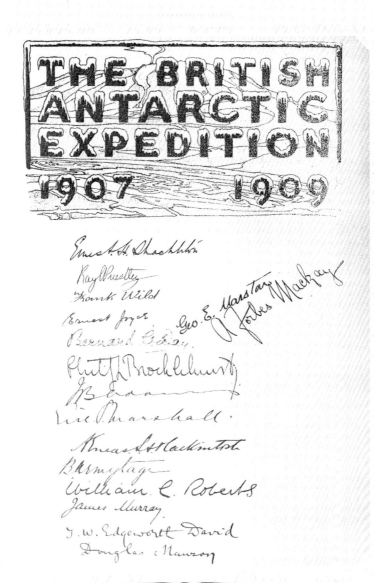

Signatures of the Shore Party on a copy of *Aurora Australis*. Bertram has signed fifth from the bottom. NATIONAL LIBRARY OF AUSTRALIA

and an amateur boxer, who didn't care much for colonials, especially when they were elderly depressives. The Boss's space where he planned next summer's polar expeditions is a little canvas-walled room aside from the front door; opposite him, Mawson's dark room walled with felt and crates of preserved fruit which had to be stored indoors.*

Overhead gas burners fed from an acetylene generator illuminate this crowded cage of 15 men that measures 19 feet wide and 33 feet long. Beneath the lamps, Wild, Joyce and Marston fiddle with the small printing press where they will produce *Aurora Australis*, the first book published in Antarctica; David and young Priestly examine their rocks; Marshall draws a map; from mending clothes to rebinding a sledge, everyone has a job. Everyone must stand a fortnightly shift as the dogsbody messman or the vital task of night watchman. Forever cheerful and encouraging Shackleton, an astute manager of men, takes no chances with cabin fever.

The hut, transported from London in disassembled sections, shuddered and shook when the great blizzards struck and temperature outside dropped to minus 40. Wire cables, thrown diagonally across the roof and ice-anchored into the permafrosted ground hold it fast. Blankets of granulated cork sandwiched by the double-timber walls and floor boards of thick tongue-and-groove hardwood, outside shielded by a bank of volcanic scoria, subdue the draft. In winter the hut's double-glazed windows are boarded up for extra warmth. There is nothing but blackness beyond unless the fluttering green and crimson curtain of an aurora draws them outside. Bertram was one who had to venture outside at 7.30 each morning, weather notwithstanding, to feed and groom the ponies. Next to the stables is the latrine where presumably everyone had to go, weather notwithstanding.

---

* Spare timber, packing and kerosene cases, and Venesta board from provision boxes were used to make furniture and bunks which in saving space Shackleton had not included in their cargo.

Mawson put his anemometer (where they recorded 100 mph winds) and Adams put his weather station on the prominence they named Flagstaff Hill above Cape Royds; every two hours someone must visit it for instrument readings. Following a lifeline stretched from the hut, in mid blizzard this is a difficult journey that no one much likes, especially when the kerosene lamp is extinguished in the wind, and the unfortunate weather man must begin his trek all over again.

The sleeping cubicles along the sides of the hut are screened by canvas curtains drawn along wire, and are given names which reflect something of the characters within. 'No.1 Park Lane' is for Marshall and Priestly. 'The Pawn Shop', distinguished by a muddle of samples and things scientific, belongs to David and Mawson. 'Rogues Retreat' is for the old Antarctic hands, Joyce and Wild, and in a tribute to Murray's diarrhoea, he and the unfortunate Priestly occupy the 'Tap Room', while 'The Gables', a place of motor manuals and paint brushes, identifies Day and Marston. Not surprisingly without adornment is 'The Shruggery' for Bertram and the Baronet. Except that after losing a toe on the Erebus climb, Brocklehurst was transferred for some weeks to The Boss's space, who himself then moved to 'The Shruggery' – possibly a good thing for Bertram.

A visit to Cape Royds is now reserved for a privileged few. Some are fare-paying tourists who, ignored by scurrying penguins and basking Weddell seals, scrunch ashore by Flagstaff Point from an ice-breaking vessel that can penetrate McMurdo Sound; others the hardy New Zealand volunteers of the Antarctic Heritage Trust who, carefully and painstakingly, have restored the hut after a lifetime of isolation amid the most unforgiving weather*. The World Monuments office listed Cape Royds as among 'the most endangered sights'. The Getty Fund, the Audrey Dance Estate (a descendant of

---

* During restoration in 2006, a woollen undershirt marked 'Bertram Armytage' was found beneath the hut.

Lady Shackleton) and other subscribers have successfully injected thousands of dollars towards its repair and maintenance.

Within its stillness and to the background of a softly moaning wind, one can imagine those voices, including Bertram's we trust, raised in a hearty chorus of 'Lead Kindly Light' to the accompaniment of a wind-up gramophone at Divine Service each Sunday morning; to the shouts of anger when Mackay tried to strangle the cook until Mawson broke them apart, after an innocently unthinking Roberts ('Bobs') dared place his booted foot on the tempermental medico's seachest. In another of the few reported conflicts in the hut, the censorious Marshall threatened to take Wild ('Franky') outside and 'hammer' him for certain intemperate remarks. Wild, one of the greatest Antarcticans, had a problem with the bottle – one of the reasons perhaps that he embraced the polar wilderness. That winter appeared 'almost over instead of just beginning' was lucky for them all wrote Priestly in commenting on 'a disagreeable fraccas'.

Much more agreeable would be lunch on Sunday when a toast was made to 'sweethearts and wives' or to celebrate a birthday or mid-winter's day (when the teetotal rule could be dispensed), possibly with community singing or poetry recital during the afternoon, listening to the gramophone or in the performance of an exceedingly amateur theatrical in which Marston ('Putty' or 'the Jester') might play the lead. If sweets were handed around Bertram should remember the occasion when he accepted one of the bullseyes sent from London by Emily Shackleton as a gift for the expedition, only to find he was biting into wood, which Marston, the practical joker, had carefully shaped and painted. When no one was watching he threw it into the fire. (But they were.)

The long table, lowered from the ceiling for Roberts' serving of the evening meal, promptly at 6.30, remained in place as a centre of nightly recreation which heard many a weighty conversation, the scrape of playing cards, the rattle of dice and roulette wheel, or the hesitant movement of a chessman – and the sighs over yet another sock to darn. From the wall, the King and Queen gazed approvingly within their frames. An advertisement for ladies' corsets seems the most public attempt at the risqué. The Boss might be known for a roving eye in London, but at Cape Royds smutty talk is not countenanced, not from any of the cross-section of manhood and experience that comprise his expedition. We have left the ladies behind, and leave it as such.

In the growing exterior darkness, Marshall sat at the table to write in his diary on 26 March. 'Shackleton had a good talk with "What What" and told him it must be his fault that he cannot get on with the men as the remaining 14 can.' And again on 2 April, 'Armytage still in an extraordinary sulky mood everyone else is getting on A.1'. Then on 13 May 'Mac and Armytage asked Shackleton re "chance of Southern journey" [referring to the Pole], received no encouragement. Ponies not allowed to be ridden any more. Shackleton fearing to tell them put up notice . . .'; though on 10 July: 'Armytage has certainly improved and taken over sole charge of the ponies . . .' At the same table, David wrote in a letter for Cara, his wife in Sydney, about 'a very nice young Victorian, educated at Cambridge, I like him immensely'.*

Nothing but quiet would descend later most evenings when David, in a voice rich with its Welsh intonation, gave his regular reading of a chapter from Dickens, to be followed at 11 o'clock with a cup of tea and biscuit, and then to bed. According to Wild, it was the only time he enjoyed hearing a Charles Dickens novel. In a paper written as an older man at Cambridge, Priestly recalled:

> Who amongst us all will have forgotten or will forget the Dickens readings which were far and away the most popular feature of the recreation of that winter. From their commencement after supper until their conclusion – often in the small hours of the morning –

---

* To Edgeworth David, aged 50, everyone in the Shore Party was 'young' including Bertram at 39.

the hut was swept with gales of laughter, while we listened to the adventures of Mr Pickwick, Sam Weller and other delightful characters of that inimitable story read in a way Dickens himself could not have surpassed. Indeed, it was difficult to allow the reader to stop and on more than one occasion the closure was put to his reading by the reminder of our leader from his cabin in the corner in no uncertain terms that it was after one o'clock and time 'all good explorers' were in bed.

Beyond midnight the hut lapsed into a measured cacophony of snores, farts and grunts of 14 sleeping men, leaving the night watchman to mind the stove, and possibly enjoy his fortnightly scrub in the collapsible canvas bath.

MIDWINTER NIGHT

The acetylene splutters and flickers,
The night comes into its own.
Outside Ambrose and Terror
Are snarling over a bone.

And this is the tale of the watchman,
Awake in the dead of night,
Tells of the fourteen sleepers
Whose snoring gives him the blight.

The revels of Eros and Bacchus
Are mingled in some of their dreams,
For the songs they gustily gurgle
Are allied to bibulous themes.

And subjects re barmaids and bottles,
Whisky and barrels of beer,
Are mixed with amorous pleadings
That sound decidedly queer.

[Shackleton, in *Aurora Australis*, Cape Royds, 1908]

CHAPTER 11

BAPTISM OF FROST

On a black winter's morning of 12 August, Shackleton left Cape Royds with Professor Edgeworth David and Bertram Armytage to test the surface of the Great Ice Barrier for his march to the Pole. The other objective was to give his two companions what he shrewdly called 'a baptism of frost'.

'It was not without feelings of unalloyed pleasure,' he wrote, 'that we turned our backs on the warm well-found hut and faced our little journey out into the semi-darkness and intense cold. But we did get a certain amount of satisfaction from the thought that at last we were actually beginning the work we had come south to undertake!' For the first five miles, Quan, the heaviest and strongest of the ponies, hauled their sledge loaded with a fortnight's provisions, including three gallons of petroleum fuel. As the sea ice of McMurdo Sound grew rougher, their support team turned back with Shackleton's telling comment, 'I did not want to run the risk of losing another pony from our sadly diminished team'.

Man-hauling was now the rule for the rest of the journey that led into a menacing shadow land (for the sun's return was still 10 days off) where, in David's words, 'a stranded 'berg loomed up like a ghostly battleship'. The 23 miles separating Cape Royds from Hut Point, where Scott had moored *Discovery* seven years before, took two days to complete – and on foot for skis, despite the Norwegian's advice, were not the British way. In the process they endured forging into paralytic winds, leaping tide cracks, heaving the burdened sledge up icy slopes, eating a hoosh prepared on the Nansen cooker and a plasmon biscuit to accompany a mug of cocoa. At minus 40 they finally struggled into their one-man sleeping bags which Shackleton preferred to the three-man variety. ('The larger bags, holding two or three men, certainly give greater warmth for the occupants warm one another, but, on the other hand, one's rest is very likely to be disturbed by the movements of a companion.') All of this was old hat to Shackleton, but for Bertram and the Prof it rapidly conveyed the meaning of 'baptism'. Knowing only three of the expedition's 15 men were 'old Antarctic hands', they recognised in their trials the privilege of being The Boss's first students taken on the road to the Pole. 'It is very desirable,' Shackleton had said, 'that all members of the expedition would have a personal experience of travelling over the ice and snow in low temperatures before the real work begins.' Shackleton's main energy might focus on reaching the Pole but he had two other expeditions to launch, both of which depended on the men who trudged beside him across the McMurdo ice. For David, the 'real work' lay in taking the Northern Party on a major journey to the South Magnetic Pole, in direction almost the opposite to that of The Boss, yet almost as far. For Bertram, 'real work' meant leadership of the Western Party which, toward the end of the year, would explore glaciers and peaks on the far side of McMurdo Sound.

The Prof's appointment was no surprise; it signalled Shackleton's immense confidence in the 50-year-old academic from Sydney University. Shackleton saw David as his greatest personal investment in the BAE, not only gaining a distinguished scientist who elevated the standing of the expedition, but also a moderating force among a disparate crowd of men jammed together in a little hut: an anticipator of problems, a calming influence when tempers rose, never lost for a story to tell, nor an ear to listen. In Shackleton's own words, he was 'a tower of strength'.

One might ask if Bertram's appointment was also Shackleton's way of casting a vote of confidence in their troubled 'Mister What-what'. He had coaxed Bertram through surviving the darkest months of winter. The four ponies restored to his care were very much alive and healthy. He quietly observed that Bertram found good comradeship among other older members, David and Frank Wild in particular, and also an understanding friend in Raymond Priestly, whose assistant he sometimes became on the young geologist's field trips at Cape Royds. David, in his concern for Bertram's wellbeing, was alert, as he later said, to their Australian comrade's 'too much introspection and brooding', yet understood him essentially as 'a simple minded, gallant, and loyal friend'. And again 'that he was a downright, good, sterling fellow and there was no one in our expedition who worked more cheerfully or more unselfishly. He was a man who did not know what fear was'. And to Priestly, he was 'one of the best'.

Bertram, in his one newspaper interview, and demonstrating his usual austerity with words, paid tribute to 'the remarkable skill and courage and tact displayed by Professor David. His pluck and energy were wonderful'. And of Shackleton, 'he was able to handle men well. He knew how to encourage them to do the utmost. We would perhaps be a little morose and gloomy and he would see to it. In about 10 minutes he would have dispelled the gloom, and have everybody laughing and happy again'. Though he spoke in the royal plural, Bertram was surely talking about himself.

They reached Hut Point on the morning of 14 August. 'After a good breakfast I took the Professor and Armytage over all the familiar ground. It was very interesting for me to revisit the old scenes. There was the place where, years before, when *Discovery* was lying fast close to the shore, we used to dig for ice that was required for fresh water. The marks of the picks and shovels were still to be seen!' What memories must have flooded back, of their ship frozen hard in Winter Quarters Bay, the prefabricated hut from Melbourne which they had pieced together to hold their stores, and that November morning close to six years before when he and 'Uncle Bill' Wilson went with Scott into unknown Antarctica. They dog sledged across the Barrier for 59 days and covered 380 miles to the south, until man and dog alike fell victim to an adverse diet. All three were smitten with scurvy and, without the dogs to help, began an agonising struggle to regain the ship. Shackleton suffered most from starvation and sickness and, for part of the time, was dragged on the sledge, a fact of which Scott made no secret. After they hobbled back to Hut Point on 3 February (1903), Scott told Shackleton that he was being invalided home. That moment of dismissal was the spark of why they stood here today. The Boss framed in the doorway of the same old hut, gazing across the same white desert of the Barrier, contemplating the same monstrous journey to reach the Pole.

Shackleton led them to the cliffs of Danger Point where the wooden cross recalled George Vince, the young seaman who had fallen to his death in the storm of January 1902, the first man lost in McMurdo Sound. At the top of nearby Crater Hill, the ever enquiring David collected rock and photographed the scene, and again along the ridge at Castle Rock until hunger pangs finally brought them down the slope to a square meal cooked within the old hut before they prepared to face the Barrier.

Away from Hut Point on the morning of 15 August, they dragged the sledge up an eight-foot slope from sea ice to reach the fixed surface of that gigantic frozen slab, larger than a kingdom. Across rough sastrugi ridges of the Great Ice Barrier they covered 12 miles in the space of eight hours. Shackleton had mixed feelings about his sampling of the Barrier surface. 'The conditions did not seem favourable for the use of the motor-car because we had already found that the machine could not go through soft snow for more than a few yards.' The tent quickly went up when a blizzard rushed in from the south, pinning them within thin shuddering fabric walls. The Prof's whiskers froze to the hood of his Burberry jacket and Shackleton placed the primus stove above his head to thaw him out. Battling the wind, goggled to beat the scourge of snow blindness, trying to unroll ice-stiff sleeping bags and assemble the Nansen cooker with unfeeling fingers were lessons in polar living that The Boss had promised.

> At 6 p.m. the thermometer showed fifty-six degrees below zero, and the petroleum used for the lamp had become milky in colour and of a creamy consistency. That night the temperature fell lower still, and the moisture in our sleeping bags from our breath and the burberries, made us very uncomfortable when the bags thawed out with the warmth of our bodies. Everything we touched was appallingly cold and we got no sleep at all.

Next morning the weather had barely improved and before another blizzard struck they turned for Hut Point and shelter. Once again, blizzard trapped them at the Discovery Hut where an inner wall built from discarded packing cases helped to stem draft and seeping snow. Knowing that they were losing condition through inactivity in the intense cold, Shackleton decided to make a run for it. At five o'clock on the morning of 22 August, the first day when the sun showed its rim above the far northern horizon, the trio marched down the ice of McMurdo Sound, determined to make no stop. Twelve hours later, and 10 days since they had left, the feeble beacon of the hut at Cape Royds awaited. 'Our comrades were delighted to see us, and we had a hearty dinner and enjoyed the luxury of a good bath,' wrote David. 'Oh, the luxury of dry blankets after a stifling wet sleeping bag!' Bertram and the Prof must have congratulated themselves; their baptism of frost accomplished.

Shackleton's journey to the Pole began from Cape Royds on 29 October. Three weeks before, the remaining party had performed much the same farewell when David, Mawson and Mackay left on their trek to the South Magnetic Pole. Except that with only four ponies remaining, these three unfortunates faced man-hauling across

1200 miles of glaciers and the lofty plateau of Victoria Land until they located that elusive point where the world's lines of magnetic force converge. They even lacked a Union Jack to fly at the Pole until Day, their resourceful mechanic, ran some handkerchiefs and ribbons together on the sewing machine. Day, incidentally, was resting a badly bruised ankle after a toboggan he shared with Bertram crashed into a hidden rock.

Bertram hoped it was his muscular strength and not just the seniority of his years that earned him a place in the journey that stood at the peak of all the BAE's ambitions. For the first five miles, with Day perched importantly at the wheel, they enjoyed the comfort of a seat on the stuttering little car, the sledge dragging behind. Then it was one-two-three heave-ho! as they leaned into the traces and began the tramp down McMurdo Sound. Fanwise, within the same bellyband harness roped to the 600 lb load, were Joyce, Marston, Brocklehurst and Priestly; Bertram would note in their puffing and grunting that though being the oldest he was also, dare he say it, the fittest of them all. Walking beside them came the Pole party itself, with the four sledge-hauling ponies enveloped in their thick woolly winter coats. The Boss led a plodding Quan, Wild with a spirited 'little Socks', Marshall with nervous young Grisi and Adams with faithful Chinaman. Each sledge bore a load averaging 650 lbs carrying provisions to last 91 days, enough they reckoned for the almost 800 miles to the Pole, and to get them back again.

They paused at Hut Point to rest and refasten their loads and pick up provisions that had been stored in the hut. Early on 3 November, with pennons flying, they were away again, entering into the challenge of the Barrier and, by some as yet unknown path, taking Queen Alexandra's flag to that coveted untrodden point at the bottom of the world. Six days later from a depot made near Minna Bluff, the support team gave three cheers as four men and their ponies merged into the enveloping snows.

Some feeling of apprehension must have stuck Bertram in

> *The success of the expedition is due mainly to Lieutenant Shackleton. He is an ideal leader. In the first place, he is a wonderful organizer. The whole of the expedition, down to the trivial details, had been carefully thought out beforehand. The organization was perfect. Everything that was needed was provided. Then, Lieutenant Shackleton was able to handle the men well. He knows how to keep them in good heart, and has a rare charm of manner and a wonderful memory. He forgets nothing that he has seen or heard. We saw a great deal of him and learned to appreciate fully his splendid abilities as a leader of men. We would be perhaps a little morose and gloomy, and Lieutenant Shackleton would see it. In about 10 minutes he would have everybody laughing and happy again.*
>
> [Bertram Armytage interviewed in Sydney, 6 April 1909.]

watching the marchers strain against the burdened sledges, each man grasping a harness to urge his pony forward. Upon reaching the Barrier the animals had plunged their hesitant hoofs into the soft snow, sometimes sinking up to their bellies; at night they shivered surprisingly, needing the protection of a hastily built snow wall and coats severely rubbed. Their weight had already given Marshall and his Grisi a close call with a hidden crevasse. One had to have confidence that The Boss knew what he was doing. As the support team turned for Hut Point, it was just as well Bertram did not know that within a month all his animals would be dead, one of exhaustion, two from maiming injuries and the fourth disappearing into a crevasse.*

Can you not hear the sea shanties from the ship anchored below on Winter Quarters Bay? Dear old Discovery Hut. Last house before the South Pole. More Antarctic history and suffering has

---

* 'If there is a paradise for ponies, ours will have some crowns in it!' (from Shackleton's lectures).

passed beneath its scarred timbers than any other heritage site you care to name.

When I was first in Antarctica 50 years ago, ice held the hut in an embalming shroud; in a way, a form of captive preservation. Nothing had disturbed the impedimenta of Scott and Shackleton since the last old explorer closed the door. Timbers within still blackened by the blubber stove, code marks on the planks telling how to put the hut together, snow heaped beneath enclosing verandahs which the Melbourne builder more expected to shelter a sheep farmer in a sweltering outback. Bertram and the Prof probably used some of the wood scattered about to build their sheltering wall. What a splendid role reversal! I have a cherished letter from Sir Douglas Mawson thanking me for a photograph of the hut, 'I well recall camping there for a few days' rest at a time during my years as a member of the first Shackleton expedition'. Members of Captain Scott's second expedition, based on Cape Evans further north, camped here while they waited for 'the Owner' to return, climbing nearby Observation Hill in a fruitless search for five distant figures trudging across the Barrier. Discovery Hut would be the first to contain their melancholy report, 'the Pole party has not returned'.

During Shackleton's second expedition (of 1914), the hut also sheltered the 10 unfortunate men of his Ross Sea party who were marooned in McMurdo Sound when an ice break-out carried their ship away. Two of them, Mackintosh and Hayward, walked out that door to make a dash for Cape Evans and were never seen again. Americans and New Zealanders of 40 years later settled by Hut Point and the Discovery Hut is accessible now, probably visited by more people in a year than all those old Antarctic hands combined. I liked it better with the memories and the mess that men like Bertram left behind.

CHAPTER 12

BRUSH WITH KILLERS

Raymond Priestly recalled the closing episode of the Western Party as the most nightmarish of his life; a frightening day that seemed to take a fortnight to live through with haunting images of killer whales with gaping jaws and razor teeth.

With Priestly and Brocklehurst as his companions, Bertram led the way on 9 December across the sea ice to the far western side of McMurdo Sound. The Boss's written instructions were to make a supply depot at Butter Point, a mere landmark amid the fast ice of the coast, awaiting David, Mawson and Mackay on the return from their far northern march. Afterwards, following Scott's charts of six years earlier, they were to ascend the Ferrar Glacier in search of fossils along the sandstone cliffs that would flank their progress as far as Depot Nunatak which was a promising field site. In a further instruction, being a confessed treasure seeker, Shackleton said they were to watch for traces of precious metals. Priestly well remembered Shackleton's question of his joining the BAE – 'Would you know gold if you saw it?'

For Priestly, the Western Party was a junior geologist's rare opportunity to snare a corner of Antarctica for himself, not overshadowed by the presence of David or Mawson. For Brocklehurst, their photographer and geologist's assistant and at almost the same age as Priestly, it was something of a consolation prize after the amputation of his big toe in the aftermath to Mount Erebus had cost him the chance of glory at the Pole. For Bertram, the older uncle figure (he 39, they 22 and 21) and proud that he was his companions' equal in fitness, it was the chance to prove himself a significant player in the expedition's achievement.

'The journey you are to undertake is by no means an easy one', wrote Shackleton to Bertram in his instructions for the Western Party, 'and the complete fulfilment and its objects will do much towards furthering the general success of the Expedition'. The letter, secure in Bertram's satchel (*see* Appendix), expressed a clear vote of reliance on the Australian's leadership:

> therefore in selecting you to command the Party I am placing a confidence in you that I consider justified after what I have seen of your work here [at Cape Royds] and when as a member of the earliest sledge journey made in the Antarctic before the winter night was over, when you were with me on the above journey.

They had, in fact, made two treks across the Sound before the Party's serious work could begin. Eight days earlier, the Arrol Johnston ferried them from Cape Royds with a 1600 lb sledge in tow. The valiant little car managed 16 miles across the sea ice before sinking to its hubs in the softening mid-summer snow. Manned by Day and Marston, it was barely able to return to the hut where, parked in a shed, it never again ventured on such a marathon mission.

Without the luxury of a motor-car seat, for the second time the Western Party had man-hauled across McMurdo Sound, three specs facing the ramparts of mountain and glacier that reared towards the clouds. On 13 December they paused at a feature called the Stranded Moraines, stretched along the tumultuous outfall of the glacier which bore the name of the Discovery expedition's geologist.*

---

* Albert Armitage, Scott's second-in-command, with Hartley Ferrar and Engineer Lt Reginald Skelton explored the glacier in 1902–1903, finding a path to the Polar Plateau.

They were assailed while making camp by a flock of skua gulls which tore with their sharp beaks at the bindings and bundles on the sledge. Seeing they had stolen 100 skua eggs, a dozen of which were cooked and the rest discarded in the snow, Bertram had to agree that the attack was not without provocation.

> The main object of your journey is geological exploration . . . After passing the area of disturbance [on the Ferrar Glacier] you are to proceed to any locality that the geologist Priestly thinks most suitable for his work always having due regard for the safety of the Party under your charge.

The mid-summer polar sun made man-hauling a misery, clogging the sledge runners in yielding snow and sometimes sinking them up to the knees, leaving their feet constantly wet. Brocklehurst wrote 'the sun beat down on us, splitting our faces and lips and one could feel one's skin crack'. They stripped to their underwear in the heat, but when he prepared to take a photograph, Brocklehurst recorded that Bertram, 'not wanting to be seen in his drawers and vest', dodged behind the sledge. On 15 December they had marched far enough up the Ferrar's sloping face to let Priestly begin his fossil hunt. Bertram found fragments of sandstone with fern-like markings which was the geologist's best reward for a frustrating day's work, and his pickings elsewhere would not get much better.

> I wish to have the most likely places for fossils examined at low altitude first . . . If it is necessary to proceed as high as Depot Nunatak you are to be specially careful as to your camping arrangements when passing through the area known as the North West area, and particularly when in the vicinity of Windy Gully. Should any member of your Party show signs of mountain sickness you are to descend to lower altitude.

On 19 December, the inevitable blizzard burst from the plateau, pinning them in the tent and, when calm returned, they faced wind-scoured patches of slippery blue ice. The vicious cold suddenly struck when shadows fell across the glacier's edge, causing the ice sheet to contract to the sound of pistol shots and shattering glass. Priestly's diary shows that he and Bertram made numerous side trips together in search of fossils. ('Spent morning rambling over mountains with Armytage and collected specimens . . . Armytage and I walked sharply from 4 to 6.') They investigated a towering promontory named Solitary Rocks but discovered it to be a peninsula jutting from the cliffs, meaning one error they could correct from Scott's old charts.

Regardless of his youth, an equanimity of temperament was Priestly's virtue which allowed him to appreciate in Bertram an interesting and likeable character, once rid of his moods and depression. ('This pm Armytage and I spent walking about and talking until dinner time, and the time passed very pleasantly.') But Brocklehurst grew increasingly dismissive of 'Mister What-what' and his military style directions, especially when the leader refused his request for an extra pannikin of water each day to clean his teeth. Between the two men a wall of silence descended, no less fixed and chilly than a grounded iceberg.

> You are to return to your depot at Butter Point reaching it not later than January the 7th 1909 and wait there keeping a lookout for the Northern Party.

In the thickening snow, Bertram announced that they must turn back if camp were to be made at Butter Point by the promised early January. Priestly reluctantly accepted that his planned exploration of Depot Nunatak lay beyond their reach. ('I was very disappointed . . . and inclined to think Armytage was over cautious, but subsequent circumstances have all combined to prove him right.') Yet for Brocklehurst it was another annoyance that he associated with Bertram's crusty management. Sometimes having to restrain the sledge with ropes, and suffering damage to the runners in the process, they began easing down the glacier, only to find that the route trapped them in a minefield of crevasses. Snow bridges crumbled beneath their boots and potholes swallowed them to the waist in freezing water. They spent 25 December at a feature named Knob Head, huddled in the wind-whipped tent to eat a Christmas dinner of tinned boneless chicken and small plum pudding – which Priestly voted 'top hole' and offered thanks to the young lady in Christchurch who had given it to Frank Wild.*

They arrived at Butter Point in time to greet the new year of 1909 but found no sign of the Northern Party for which they carried another set of Shackleton's instructions. For nearly three weeks they waited, though Bertram agreed to some local excursions including the Stranded Moraines on 6 January where Priestly added 250 lb of rock to their sledge. Another trek around the sea ice led into the weird moon-like phenomenon of the dry valleys where Brocklehurst let off steam by climbing the improbably named Harbour Heights. Clearly the final 10 days of enforced idleness did not fit well with the three men. 'Brocklehurst practising waltz steps out on the floe . . . Armytage is strolling about by himself.' The entries in Priestly's diary hint of the rising frustration of waiting for a Northern Party which, for all they knew, could have been swallowed in a crevasse.

> When you meet the Northern Party you are to hand the enclosed instructions to Professor David. If Professor David has been lost during the expedition of his Party, Mawson will be in command and the orders are to be handed to him.

---

* 'We must remember to give one of the pot-holed sandstones to Wild for the New Zealand girl who gave him the plum pudding.' (Priestly's diary.)

Brocklehurst's graphic dream that all the ponies were dead (correct, but not for the man-hauling Northern Party) and David and Mawson were down a crevasse (frequently correct) did not help matters. The lanky young baronet, used to having his own way and more likely giving orders than receiving them, met with another refusal when he wanted them to move camp into the Dry Valley. Like heating an extra pannikin of water to clean one's teeth, marching to the Dry Valley was a waste of resources, and also outside instructions, and the former Dragoons cavalry officer was having none of it. So the unfortunate Priestly found himself continuing in the bizarre role of communicator between two men who, in the frozen wilderness of deep Antarctica, refused to exchange a spoken word.

> Should the Northern Party not arrive at Butter Point by the 20th of January you are to take your Party to Glacier Tongue if the ice permits.

By the third week in January, Bertram's thinking needed to change. He had tried repeatedly to heliograph Murray, now in charge at Cape Royds, for information but without response. Knowing that the ship must be close to reappearing and that David and his comrades might well be safely aboard, he took the fateful decision on 24 January that they should move. Leaving most of the supplies at Butter Point, they made for the edge of the sea ice where *Nimrod* would be easily seen and they, hopefully, seen by it. Bertram surveyed the extent of a tide crack along the shore and decided everything looked normal enough to strike camp and put up the tent. They ate a meal of hoosh, coffee and a chocolate bar and, tired from their latest spell of man-hauling, climbed into the sleeping bags and fell asleep.

Priestly was first awake next morning and left the tent at seven o'clock to check the weather and their surroundings. All he saw, and all around them, was open water. Bertram and Brocklehurst awakened to his cry: 'We've broken out – we're on a floe drifting!' In the tidal current they were being washed down McMurdo Sound; beyond the Sound lay the iceberg-filled Ross Sea and, unless they could escape – oblivion. A thumping noise in the night that had dimly disturbed their slumber began to make dreadful sense. A pod of killer whales circled the floe, intent on dislodging the dark shapes above which surely must be basking seals, their intended morning meal.

In the frantic moments that followed they traced the perimeter of the floe, searching for an escape route and saw only a widening gap of open water between themselves and the western shore where the pursuing killers dived and spouted, sometimes throwing their huge heads against the sides of the floe to spy them out with their wicked piggy eyes. According to Priestly 'one of them bumped directly beneath our tent, cracking the ice in all directions'. To combat the slow freezing of their limbs on the floe's windswept surface, they took shelter again in the tent, cooked a hurried meal of hoosh and pondered their options – which were exactly nil, unless one decided was it better to drown or be eaten? No sign of the ship; nothing much more for food because of the stores left at Butter Point. Bertram decided they could survive on the floe for two more days and put them on half rations – in a sense a futile step? Bertram and Brocklehurst at last spoke, mutually agreeing that Englishmen should be united in the face of a common peril. They shook hands, and one assumes, Priestly gave a sigh of relief. All three collapsed into an exhausted sleep, careless of the renewed hammering as the killers surrounding the floe prepared for a coup de grace.

Close to midnight, Bertram awoke to the sensing of something different in the movement of the floe. He threw off the sleeping bag and, as he later wondered, directed as if by some unseen force, quickly surveyed their position. About 200 yards ahead, a fringe of ice jutted from the fast ice of the shore; the drift of the floe had changed, maybe with the impacted current, from south to easterly. In a few moments they might graze the fast ice and briefly make a bridge.

He shouted to the others to collapse the tent, grab the sledge and be ready to jump. The top of the projecting ice, in reality the end of the glacier tongue, was a man's height above them as they came alongside. A bare few yards of the frozen surfaces scraped together and in another minute or less, the joining would cease. 'The snout of the glacier was some six feet above us', Brocklehurst recorded. 'As it [the floe] touched, we leapt across the gap and scrambled up the slope, dragging what we could with us. Some kit fell off as the sledge was about perpendicular and hurriedly packed, so Raymond and Armytage held me by the heels as I collected the odds and ends . . .' and 'the killers were all around us at the foot of the glacier, great ugly brutes deprived of their unusual breakfast'.

In Bertram's report to Shackleton, we find a somewhat austere record of that desperate drama, but Priestly's diary added detail to the description. 'The sledge tipped over enough to tilt a couple of oilcans, boots, finnesko and some cakes of chocolate out . . . which Brocklehurst hurled up indiscriminately, one just missing my nose and the other which hit Armytage.'

By three in the morning they had retreated to the security of Butter Point. Bertram set up his heliograph to again signal their whereabouts, at first failing to raise a reply. But *Nimrod*'s watch spied the momentary flash of light from far across the Sound and a new bearing was shouted to the helmsman. The three and their sledge, still holding Priestly's rocks, were lifted aboard ship at three o'clock on the afternoon of 26 January. In his log, Captain Evans entered that 'a chill more than the ice' was evident between Brocklehurst and Armytage. In reality, the renewed bond of friendship between the two men had lasted barely 24 hours. 'In a sentimental point of view', the *Nimrod*'s master wrote, 'the fate of this reconciliation was deplorable but the incident demonstrated in a striking way how queer these people had become under the influence of prolonged and trying association with one another'.

> I trust to your discretion . . . feeling sure that you will successfully carry out the object of the journey.

The progress of the Western Party is detailed in these extracts from Priestly's diary:

21/12/1908
(Crossing between Solitary Rocks and Granite Bluff towards Obelisk Mountain.)
6.45 pm. We had some difficulty in finding a camp and are now waiting Armytage's report having found no snow patches ourselves ... Armytage has come back reporting no snow, but a way up on to the main glacier surface has been found and we are going to off-load, pull up and make for the sub-medial moraine. Another disadvantage is the impossibility of getting to Depot Nunatak. The only place where fossils have been found and complying with the commands which Armytage has to carry out.
11.00 pm. Armytage and myself have taken advantage of the weather to leave Brocklehurst in charge of the camp and walk down to the north end of Solitary Rocks. We have followed the bulge of the glacier round and have definitely proved the Solitary Rocks to be a peninsular joined by the main north wall of the glacier by an isthmus of granite at least 1,000 ft. high.

24/12/1908
6.30 pm. Hoosh time. Armytage and I climbed up the slope behind the tent after lunch and reached a height of 5,800 ft. by his aneroid. [They found lichens which Priestly described in detail.]

25/12/1908
... excellent camp up in a sheltered situation for Christmas Day. Lunch Garibaldi biscuits and jelly, for dinner potted boneless chicken and a small plum pudding.

26/12/1908
7.30 am. Armytage dreamed that Shackleton and he had a row, because no letters had come on the *Nimrod*.

1.30 pm. Lunch

I still think that the only chance of finding fossils in a short time in the Beacon Sandstone is to go straight up to Depot Nunatak, and examine the carbonaceous layers there. I was very disappointed when I was told that we could not go there and was inclined to think Armytage over-cautious, but subsequent circumstances have all combined to prove him right.

6.00 pm. Dinner

. . . was unable to go far this afternoon as weather is very thick and there is evidently a snowstorm raging above us. This morning Armytage and I stripped the sledge and examined the runners.

27/12/1908

Armytage and I owing to the way our spikes have blunted and worn away, have instituted a novelty in footgear for we are wearing finnesko crampons over ski boots, and with great success too.

Opinions are much divided as to the time it will take to get to Butter Point. Armytage wishes to give the same time to get back as we took to get out. Brocklehurst said this morning he thought it would take a d— sight longer to get down the slopes than even Armytage thinks, while I think myself that we shall be much quicker, weather permitting, even with the broken sledge.

3.30 pm. We camped at a height of 2700ft (4300 ft by Armytage's aneroid.)

29/12/1908

6.00 pm. . . . Still thick as a hedge . . .

Our work is divided as follows – Brocklehurst puts snow on the tent at each camp and makes that secure. I see to all the food and water distribution and deal out the ingredients for the hoosh, biscuits, milk, tea and cocoa, and Armytage cooks.

30/12/1908

Wind surface was covered by 3 inches of soft snow . . . [which] effectually veiled all but the biggest of the obstacles in our course.

The ice all the way down has been seamed with drainage channels . . . and the surface was honeycombed with boulder holes, l, 2 or even 3 ft. deep and full or partly full of water. Each of us has been in halfway up to the knee dozens of times although Armytage has naturally suffered most being first man. The sledge has illustrated my remarks to Armytage about shortening and heightening the load, by capsizing seven times and no sooner do our finnesko and clothes get dry than they are wet through again.

1/1/1909
[They reach Butter Point.]
It will be a rotten spot to stay if we have to remain here long to wait for the others, and Armytage has definite order to wait at Butter Point, and is not likely to be persuaded into taking the responsibility of shifting into Dry Valley. It only shows what a difference three letters can make for if the orders had said 'about Butter Point' all would have been all right . . . I shall consider every day spent here an entire waste of time.

3/1/1909
This pm. Armytage and I spent walking about and talking until dinner time and the time passed very pleasantly. Armytage and I struck a good idea this am. This morning we went collecting icicles off the snow cornice and secured a splendid supply of pure fresh water ice. The consequence is our meals and occasional drinks are much improved in quality, and we are also saving oil by using the ice rather than snow. I am also using bits of the thinner icicles to suck and supply the water for washing my teeth so it has proved a good idea all round!

4/1/1909
Armytage and I walked sharply from 4 to 6.

5/1/1909
Drying clothes.

6/1/1909

Have decided to move on and collect from the Stranded Moraines, taking with us next week's food bag and a ton of biscuits. It is intended that we should get there today, stay, collect tomorrow and back at Butter Pt on the 8th.

Today being Jan 6th, I have fulfilled my promise to Armytage that the food should last until this date without touching the depots at Butter Pt.

7/1/1909

Spent morning rambling over the mountains with Armytage and collecting specimens.

8/1/1909

Brocklehurst feeling seedy and Armytage not well, has felt bad for several days. Cause unknown.

Armytage made another attempt to heliograph Murray [at Cape Royds] this afternoon about 4.30–5 pm. But without success.

10/1/1909

Armytage and I tried to attract Murray from high up on the ice slab this pm. But without any success.

12/1/1909

. . . Are making for Dry Valley . . . and intend being back here by 14th. Neither Northern party nor ship in sight.

13/1/1909

6.30 pm. This pm Armytage and I followed the moraines up 3 or 4 miles and reached a height of over 800 ft and the kenyte, basalt and tuff fragments all became more and more common. After lunch we start our return to B. P. in accordance with Armytage's wish to be back there by the time the Professor mentions in his letter to me. [Professor David's letter specified 25 January.]

14/1/1909

Armytage and I strolled about . . . and discussed . . . my offer to volunteer as staying down here another year in case of the non-arrival of the Northern or Southern party before the latest date when the ship must leave for home. In case of this happening, he promised to call at Tewkesbury and give some account of me and execute any commissions.

A sixpenny copy of *The Virginian* has been read by all three of us, and Armytage and myself twice – and has afforded a good deal of fun. [Priestly had a 'small library' with him.] Armytage and Priestly also read Darwin's *Voyage of the Beagle*. We both got some very useful information out of it, he on hunting and I on geology.

16/1/1909

All three very worn tempers. At noon today Armytage had a good opportunity to attempt helioing Murray and he made the most of it, staying up there from 12 noon to 12.40 pm but he got no reply and could see no sign of a ship.

19/1/1909

Armytage has spent an hour trying to helio Murray.

21/1/1909

Brocklehurst practising waltz steps out on the floe . . . and Armytage is strolling about by himself. [The monotony of waiting is getting them down.]

23/1/1909

Last night all the floe up to the Stranded Moraines went out, and took us with it and now we are as near death as we can be.

24/1/1909

3.00 am. Safe back on Butter Point after 24 hours adrift on the floe. The killer whale lives round about the pack ice and breaks it up by bumping it in order to get the animals off it for food. Floe within 150 yards of the Point, and still moving on, and half an hour later Armytage heard a grinding noise and at once turned out and found ice hard up against the Point. He shouted to us and ran back towards us, but before he had time to reach us we had the bags up . . . the sledge tipped over enough to tilt a couple of oil cans, boots, finnesko and some cakes of chocolate out, and Brocklehurst hurled these up indiscriminately, one passing within an inch of my nose and another hitting Armytage.

I have never spent a day that seemed as much a fortnight. May I never have such an experience again. I shall dream of killer whales for weeks.

Spotted ship at 11.30 and were picked up by her before lunch.

29/1/1909

Brocklehurst and Armytage living on board ship since yesterday.*

True to his style, Bertram's report of the Western Party's progress did not dwell upon the brush with nasty death (*see* Appendix). His own ending of his life he would reserve for the Melbourne Club, and for the headlines.

---

* One assumes that Captain F. P. Evans who had commanded *Koonya* on the first southward voyage and then took command of *Nimrod* in the second voyage, heard from Priestly about the falling-out between Bertram and Brocklehurst. In notes on his voyage, Captain Evans continued: 'They were university men in the company of another graduate and both well-bred. Unmannerliness so primitive was the symptom in their cases of that nervous ill-health which afflicts in varying degrees all the members of a little community condemned to the most irksome intimacy by confinement through the long months of a polar night.'

And in another place, commenting on the men he found assembled at Cape Royds: 'They were a mixed lot inordinately jealous of one another, and rather ill-naturedly sceptical of what those still absent on sledging adventures might achieve.' However the Shore Party at Cape Royds did not take kindly to Evans's assertion that in Shackleton's absence he was now in command. This reaction may have coloured the way they viewed him.

CHAPTER 13

THE HEROES

Edgeworth David Avenue spans the well-dressed suburbs of Hornsby, Waitara and Wahroonga on the northern side of Sydney. It is long and straight, flanked by many more big houses and lush gardens than when the distinguished Professor of Geology moved to 49 Burdett Street, Hornsby, in the years of his retirement. At the University of Sydney, the headquarters of the geology department are lodged in the Edgeworth David Building; on the South Maitland coalfield, a park and memorial recall Edgeworth David's discoveries. Mawson is the name of the first Antarctic continental base established by Australia in the post-war years; Mawson's was the face familiar on the $100 banknote. In Canberra, a whole suburb is named after Douglas Mawson; numerous streets throughout the land bear his name, not to speak of Adelaide where the achievements of a favourite citizen are honoured in university and museum. Should you visit the Canberra headquarters of the Australian Academy of Science, next to a building that remarkably resembles a grounded flying saucer, take a stroll to the adjoining administrative block. There, in a simple frame, is the tattered flag that David, Mawson and Mackay flew at 72°25'S. 155°16'E., their nearest approach to the elusive South Magnetic Pole; one of the great moments of Antarctic exploration, hidden from public gaze on an office wall.

Nine days after their Butter Point rendezvous, *Nimrod* returned to the search, as Shackleton directed, for the returning Northern Party. Bertram was on deck that morning of 3 February when Arthur Harbord, officer of the watch, spied a flag fluttering above a small green triangle perched on an icy slope of the Victoria Land coast. They fired two detonators and waited. Secure if not snug in the warmth of this faithful ship, Bertram could treasure a memory sufficient to revive any man's drooping spirits of being a participant in some of the grandest exploits Antarctica was ever likely to boast. He was about to learn more. At a feature named Relief Inlet, beyond the northern edge of the vast Drygalski Glacier, safe and well enough considering their experiences, they found the missing David, Mawson and Mackay.

The appointed pick-up place was 'somewhere' along the 200 miles of the Ross Sea's western shore; January was now past and for an anxious Captain Frederick Pryce Evans, master of the *Nimrod*'s second voyage, after one close encounter with a hidden shoal this was to be the last sweep through the fog and iceberg clutter of a risky coast. By the ultimate stroke of good fortune, for which they could thank *Nimrod*'s first officer, J. K. Davis, who persuaded his captain to make a pass behind a nest of 'bergs which they had avoided before, the tiny flag came into view.

As the report of the detonators rolled back from towering ice walls, three figures emerged from the tent, waving frantically and running down the slope towards their rescuers. The first to reach the ice edge spoke in an unmistakable Scots' accent. 'Mawson's fallen into a crevasse,' Mackay cried, ' – and we reached the Magnetic Pole!' In the excitement of cheers and clapping from the ship, no one noticed that a hidden crevasse had claimed Mawson in mid stride. Again it was a quick-thinking Davis who led Bertram and Brocklehurst and members of the crew to the rescue, bearing coiled rope and lengths of timber. While the others held to his harness, Davis descended through the collapsed snow bridge and found Mawson, shaken yet unhurt, some 18 feet down, crouched on a small ledge that had saved him from disappearing into the cold sea water below.

Heroes they might be, but the trio were commanded to take a bath and change their clothes before being admitted to the ward room where hot food was waiting. Bertram was one of the small group who watched them unleash their ravenous appetites, as only polar explorers can, and heard the account of a march covering 1260 miles across 124 days, much of it spent above 7000 feet where breathing on the bleak plateau was painful; crevasse falls were frequent, blizzards were merciless, the flag was raised at the Pole for the King – and through it all, there was man-hauling the deadweight sledges. In the march for the Magnetic Pole, they scattered names across the unknown wilderness of Victoria Land. Near the dominant white dome of the slumbering volcano, Mount Melbourne at 76 degrees South, they named Mount Armytage and Mount Brocklehurst, and left them standing apart in frigid silence.*

In the slow-moving days of mid February as the men went about the dreary task of loading the fruits of their exploration and packing belongings under a gradually increasing chill, and with ice more plentiful in McMurdo Sound and their 24-hour sun perceptibly lower in the sky, all consciousness focused on the one question that mattered: where was The Boss and the men he had led to the South Pole? *Nimrod*'s return to Cape Royds on 5 January had been welcomed beyond measure, but not so much the assertion of Captain Evans, who had been *Koonya*'s master on the hazardous first voyage south as far as the pack ice, that in Shackleton's absence he was now the expedition's commander. It was an intrusion the Shore Party members must have resented, seeing Shackleton had deputised James Murray as leader, but they could not do much about it while Evans captained the ship that was to carry them away from a second Antarctic winter.

---

* Mount Armytage, 1855 m standing N of Mawson Glacier at 76°02'S and 160°45'E in Victoria Land and nearby Mount Brocklehurst at 76°08'S and 161°27'E (*Antarctic Gazetteer*).

The return of the Southern Party, now seriously overdue, was the one issue that kept *Nimrod* at Cape Royds; but for how long could they risk the spreading ice in McMurdo Sound? Earlier in the expedition, discussions had been held on the membership of a second-year team, for whom additional supplies had been purchased in New Zealand to be used if necessary in waiting for Shackleton at Hut Point, and with Mawson agreeing to stay as leader. Mackay, always short-fused in his tolerance of colonials (he called them 'foreigners'), protested that the team should have a 'British' stamp and Priestly, who had asked Bertram to take messages home for him ('Colonials are in power', he wrote), and Day and Mackintosh were added to the list. When an able-bodied Bertram put his own name forward, one might expect it would be smartly dismissed for the reason of his being one of the expedition's few married men, and with family, and now in his 40th year. Yet the records suggest B. Armytage remained among those who pledged themselves to waiting through another polar winter. What this says about how he balanced his undoubted loyalty to Shackleton against the duty of returning home to a wife and daughter was never put to the test.

One who has lived through a similar experience readily understands the sentiments of the BAE in wanting to escape the cold and darkness of an Antarctic winter. My own memory reaches back to the 1958 story I wrote for the Australian and overseas press:

> McMurdo Sound (Antarctica) – In sight of a hut that Captain Scott used on his last tragic dash to the Pole we are marooned in Antarctica, hoping for a ship to take us out. No planes can get in and none can get out. Not 200 yards from the hut where I am writing this story the sea is coming back into McMurdo Sound. The ice airfield of Operation Deep Freeze which only a few days ago held massive Globemaster transports is breaking up and drifting away.
>
> 18 men living in blizzardly isolation of the South Pole 800 miles from here, are cut off for the winter. Not so far in Deep

Freeze experience has the McMurdo ice been known to break up so early, so suddenly and so treacherously. Half an hour before the last parachute supply drop of the season was due to leave for the Pole the alarm was given that the ice was going out. By loud speakers all 70 outgoing members of the summer support team and International Geophysical Year scientists were ordered to board the final ready and waiting Globemaster. The scenes that followed were reminiscent of the best traditions of a Hollywood adventure movie as men streamed out of the huts hauling baggage, zipping up clothes, pulling on hats, throwing gear aboard revving trucks and hurrying to the helicopter take-off pad.

It is growing lonely in McMurdo now – the place they call the Crossroads of Antarctica – biggest and one of the most southerly bases in all the Polar continent. Last week the Antarctic sun set for the first time this season and snowflakes drifted on the base from the slopes of 12,000-foot Mount Erebus, the only active volcano in Antarctica which is but 30 miles from here. A husky is howling outside the door tonight; drift covers Observation Hill where they watched for a Pole party* that never returned; the barking of seals comes faintly on the wind, and I hear the sound of crunch and crumble as hundreds of tons of ice fracture and float away on the Ross Sea. We are waiting for the icebreaker to get us out.

---

* Captain Scott as well as Wilson, Bowers, Oates and Evans died on return from the South Pole in March 1912. They found that the Norwegians, led by Roald Amundsen, had reached the Pole a month before them.

Bertram Armytage emerges from an exploratory shaft dug into one of Cape Royds'
frozen lakes. He had a lucky escape when released water suddenly gushed up the hole.

Top left: Shackleton took no furniture to Antarctica but used Vanesta board from packing cases to provide the expedition's bunks, chairs and tables.
CATHERINE BURKE

Above left: Abandoned kennels outside the hut are a reminder that dogs were not favoured by Shackleton, yet may have proved of more value to him than the disappointing ponies. CATHERINE BURKE

Right: A typical cubicle in the winter quarters hut in which two men slept and stored their belongings.
A. W. ALLEN PHOTO ALBUMS,
STATE LIBRARY OF NSW

Top: The winter quarters hut at Cape Royds where 15 men lived through the blizzardly winter of 1908. A. W. ALLEN PHOTO ALBUMS, STATE LIBRARY OF NSW

Above: Shackleton purchased 10 Manchurian ponies from China but their number was reduced to four by the time the expedition was ready to begin serious exploration. A. W. ALLEN PHOTO ALBUMS, STATE LIBRARY OF NSW

Top: The Arrol Johnston motor hauling a laden sledge across the ice; Shackleton hoped the pioneer vehicle might cover long distances, but thick snow soon bogged the wheels. A. W. ALLEN PHOTO ALBUMS, STATE LIBRARY OF NSW

Above: When the motor car failed in thick snow, expedition members faced the task of man-hauling the heavy sledges across hundreds of miles. A. W. ALLEN PHOTO ALBUMS, STATE LIBRARY OF NSW

T.W. EDGEWORTH. DAVID. JUNE 7

Above: A Marston study of Professor Edgeworth
David. NATIONAL LIBRARY OF AUSTRALIA

Right: The Western Party camped beneath the cliffs of the Ferrar Glacier in December, 1908. 'The journey you are to undertake is by no means an easy one', Shackleton wrote to the leader, Bertram Armytage. A. W. ALLEN PHOTO ALBUMS, STATE LIBRARY OF NSW

Below: On 25 December, the descending party huddled in their tent at Knob Head to eat a Christmas dinner of tinned boneless chicken and a small plum pudding given by a girl in Christchurch. A. W. ALLEN PHOTO ALBUMS, STATE LIBRARY OF NSW

Below right: The mid-December temperature on the glacier turned uncomfortably hot. 'We are stripped to our underwear', Brocklehurst soon wrote, 'we can feel our skin crack'. A. W. ALLEN PHOTO ALBUMS, STATE LIBRARY OF NSW

Left: Unfriendly relations developed between the Western Party and a local skua gull population after 100 eggs were taken from their nests, with the sledge bindings suffering from irate beaks. A. W. ALLEN PHOTO ALBUMS, STATE LIBRARY OF NSW

Below: The Western Party about to be picked up after surviving a drifting ice floe and the menace of killer whales. The photo was taken from *Nimrod* on 26 January 1909 while searching the McMurdo coast. A. W. ALLEN PHOTO ALBUMS, STATE LIBRARY OF NSW

The Southern Party raises Queen Alexandra's flag at its nearest point to the South Pole on 9 January 1909. Shackleton stands next to the flag with two of his three companions Wild, Marshall and Adams. A. W. ALLEN PHOTO ALBUMS, STATE LIBRARY OF NSW

Above: With flags and pennants flying, the Southern Party stands ready to begin the march across the Great Ice Barrier. One of the figures is Bertram Armytage, a member of the support team. NATIONAL LIBRARY OF AUSTRALIA

Top right: A frame at the Australian Academy of Science, Canberra, contains the home-made flag that the Northern Party flew on their quest for the South Magnetic Pole. The photo shows them camped in the vicinity of the Pole on a trek of 1200 miles (1920 km) across Victoria Land. The figures are Mackay, Edgeworth David and Mawson. DALE BUDD

Right: The Discovery Hut, dating from Captain Scott's first expedition of 1901, where Bertram sheltered with Shackleton and David on his 'baptism of frost' into the Antarctic winter. The author's first view of the hut taken 50 years ago shows the interior filled with ice and the explorers' baggage strewn around the walls. AUTHOR'S COLLECTION

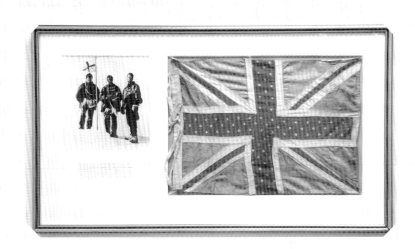

Top left: Professor Edgeworth David. Aged 50, the University of Sydney geologist was the BAE's oldest member and, in Shackleton's words, 'a tower of strength'. NATIONAL LIBRARY OF AUSTRALIA

Top right: Frank Wild, a veteran of Antarctica's heroic age and a friend of Bertram Armytage. NATIONAL LIBRARY OF AUSTRALIA

Above: The BAE hut at Cape Royds has now been restored to its original condition and, under strict preservation precautions, it is accessible to tourists from ice-breaking ships that penetrate McMurdo Sound. CATHERINE BURKE

Top left: Sir Philip Brocklehurst, who was at odds with Bertram Armytage's leadership of the Western Party. Brocklehurst's mother subscribed £2000 to have the young baronet join the BAE.
AUSTRALIAN ANTARCTIC DIVISION

Top right: Bertram Armytage aboard *Nimrod* on the voyage home from Cape Royds. His friends, Professor David and Raymond Priestly, would remember him as 'a simple-minded, gallant and loyal friend – one of the best' and 'a down-right good and sterling fellow'.
AUSTRALIAN ANTARCTIC DIVISION

Right: Raymond Priestly, the young student geologist recruited by Shackleton who asked him 'Would you know gold if you saw it?' Priestly, a famous polar figure, later became the first salaried vice-chancellor of the University of Melbourne.
MAWSON CENTRE, SOUTH AUSTRALIAN MUSEUM

Opposite page, inset: Shackleton's hut at Cape Royds is 'an historic monument' declares a plaque attached to the wall by the heritage restoration teams. CATHERINE BURKE

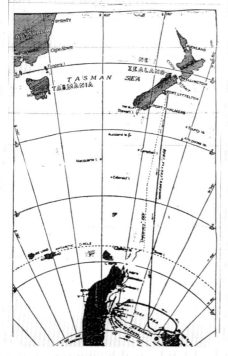

THE SYDNEY MORNING HERALD, WEDNESDAY, MARC.

BACK FROM THE ICE.

THE NIMROD'S RETURN.

PARTY ALL WELL AND VIGOROUS.

RETICENCE REGARDING DISCOVERIES.

"WHO WON THE FIGHT?"

Above: Marston's sketch of Shore Party members, with Professor Edgeworth David in the foreground holding the camera. Bertram is the second figure from the left. *AURORA AUSTRALIS,* NATIONAL LIBRARY OF AUSTRALIA

Left: Newspaper headlines announce the success of the BAE. AUTHOR'S COLLECTION

Above: Probably the BAE's last assembly when members met for dinner at a London hotel. The Boss – now Sir Ernest Shackleton – stands at the table head while Bertram, partly obscured, is on the far right.
AUSTRALIAN ANTARCTIC DIVISION

Left: A special BAE postmark was issued by New Zealand postal authorities for the stamps which Shackleton took to Antarctica.
PETER CRANWELL

Top: Como, the National Trust property in South Yarra, displays Bertram Armytage's medals from the Boer War and Antarctica. Prized exhibits are the Polar Medal, awarded to Bertram in London by King Edward VII, and a polar medallion sent from the King of the Belgians — a reminder of the Armytage family's connection with Belgium itself. AUTHOR'S COLLECTION

Above: An austere headstone marks the grave of Bertram Armytage at Boroondara Cemetery, Melbourne. The inscription, placed by his widow, makes no mention of wife, daughter or Antarctica. AUTHOR'S COLLECTION

CHAPTER 14

ESCAPE

Since leaving Hut Point on 3 November, the more optimistic expectations would have the Southern Party back at the Discovery Hut, the appointed place of rendezvous, by late January. Shackleton's basic calculations put the Pole at 859 miles distant from Cape Royds and, to remain safely within the allocated provisions, they needed to travel at an average of 19 miles each day. Yet Bertram and others of the support team well knew from the evidence of a week's slow progress that the ponies had limited them to seven miles daily. Surely a big catch-up would be needed to stay within the safety margin – which did not allow for the inevitable delays of crevasses, sastrugi, storms and thick snow. Shackleton had hoped to find the Pole at the same elevation as the Barrier surface, but what if he was in error and mountains blocked their path?

Fears for the party's survival grew serious by the time they were two weeks overdue. Ernie Joyce, one of Shackleton's old comrades from the *Discovery*, twice took a dog team with a sledge of provisions across the Barrier to their Bluff depot with the hope of intercepting a home-bound party. Joyce was the expedition's appointed member who laboured to form the dogs into a sledging team whereas others seemed to regard them as playful pets which made Cape Royds more homely. But by 20 February he was forced to retreat to Hut Point with nothing to report, except that his own small expedition, in battling through snow drifts, had counted 127 crevasses in 37 miles. He could also report their survival was due in large measure to the dogs, rapid in the traces and pulling the sledge across snow bridges where a heavier animal would be likely to fall. What if, he must wonder – what if The Boss had chosen dogs instead of ponies; just as Nansen might be entitled to ask, what if they had chosen to glide on skis? Mawson recorded similar feelings.

Escape from Antarctica was uppermost on Captain Evans' mind when he brought *Nimrod* back to Cape Royds to continue loading in the event of a sudden departure. When the weather turned sour, he sheltered the ship in the lee of Glacier Tongue, roughly halfway in the 23 miles separating Cape Royds and Hut Point. Shackleton had directed the keeping of a camp at Hut Point and stationing a watch on nearby Observation Hill, but due to the divided command between ship and shore, in the crucial days of late February neither was properly done.

Meanwhile, on 27 February, the Southern Party had reached within 100 miles of Hut Point. Returning exhausted and under-nourished in man-hauling across the Barrier, their passage through heavy drift, sastrugi ridges and crevasses brought them to the point of collapse. The doctor, Marshall, had fallen to dysentery and stomach paralysis which he blamed on eating the Fortnum & Mason cake intended for Brocklehurst's 21st birthday. Wild, who was Shackleton's main support, had also succumbed to dysentery which he attributed to the frozen meat of a dead pony. Shackleton's spectre was 1 March, just 36 hours away. This was the date he had set, so late in the season with the threat of McMurdo freezing over, for *Nimrod* to leave Cape Royds. Leaving Adams at the tent to care for the stricken Marshall and accompanied by Wild, carrying only a compass, tent, sleeping bags and a little food, Shackleton began a forced march to reach Hut Point before another day had passed. Pressure ridges and a wide crevasse belt forced them to make a delaying detour to the east and not until late in the evening of 28 February did they climb the slope to the Discovery Hut.

A message tacked to the window told that *Nimrod* had come and gone from Winter Quarters Bay and would shelter at Glacier Tongue until 26 February. Nothing else was said. It was now two days after, yet just possible that the ship had not gathered the Shore Party and departed. The pair tried to make a beacon by setting fire to the remains of Scott's old magnetic hut but in the intense cold, nothing would come alight; next they tried fastening a flag to Vince's cross on the ridge where Scott's young seaman had plunged to his death, but their fingers were too numb to tie a knot. Near to collapse, they stumbled back to the hut, made a weak hoosh on an improvised stove, rolled themselves in a strip of discarded roofing felt and spent sleepless hours wondering if, just by a day, they had missed the ship.

'Fortitudine vincimus' (by endurance we conquer), Shackleton's family motto, called for no surrender. On 1 March, sufficiently revived after the meal and a few hours' pause, they once more attempted a signal and the magnetic hut began to burn. The flag was tied around the cross with more success and they waited and hoped. The sound of a steam whistle cut through the driving wind. Evans had brought *Nimrod* back one more time to leave a wintering-over team who would await the Southern Party or search for their bodies. Instead they saw two men waving at them from the shore of Winter Quarters Bay, where the road to the Pole began. Bertram was one of that cheering, hand-shaking and back-thumping company who surrounded Shackleton and Wild as they climbed aboard. For Wild, 'no happier sight ever met the eyes of man'.

The Boss would not stay. After a quick meal of bacon and fried bread, and recruiting Mawson, Mackay and McGillion, a crew member, to help (but leaving Wild as a back-stop in case of emergency) he was away. Two comrades were stranded in a tent far across the Barrier and in the dwindling time left to them, he was the only one who knew the path. When they returned with Marshall and Adams two days later, courage and compassion had carried him through 55 hours without sleep.

In the meantime, Evans removed *Nimrod* to Cape Royds to complete the stowing of the expedition's belongings. Bertram was again reminded of the slender margin by which they survived when rising seas dashed a loaded boat making for the ship with 12 men aboard against the jagged ice of Back Door Bay. Ropes lowered by those waiting on the cliff above helped to save them from the waves. Brocklehurst was among the rescued company and this time he might have been glad to see Bertram's face. Possibly from here on their relationship improved.

Calmness and self-control were qualities which Bertram would remember of The Boss. He had brought Marshall and Adams back to Hut Point on 3 March, only to find their ship unbelievably absent. Amid thickening ice, and with time running out, fury and defeat might have consumed a lesser man; for Shackleton the only issue was in bringing *Nimrod* back as quickly as possible which he and Mackay achieved by pump-shipping (urinating) into a carbide flare container where moisture was necessary to set it alight. Mackintosh, the one-eyed sailor of their earlier voyage, saw the blaze from nine miles to the north and called for steam. In the gathering gloom of a polar midnight the waiting party came aboard *Nimrod* on 4 March, and Shackleton gave the order to leave. Bertram listened to how the ponies once under his care had died; all within a month of sending them away with a smack and a cheer. Chinaman, Grisi and Quan, snow blinded, injured or worn out, dispatched with a bullet, each out of sight of the others behind the tent, their meat butchered, some stored, some loaded all bloody upon the sledge. Willing little Socks was the exception; last to go, in the blink of an eye, hurtled into a crevasse on the great glacier, almost taking Wild and a loaded sledge with him into 'the black, bottomless pit'.

In *Nimrod*'s tiny wardroom, Bertram and his comrades heard from cracked lips and hoarse voice the saga of the Southern Party's march of 1700 miles across 128 days. With the loss of their ponies the four were forced into man-hauling. On 26 November they passed the furthest south of the National Antarctic Expedition: at 380 miles from Hut Point, Shackleton could exorcise haunting memories of his trek with Scott and Wilson of six years before.

Much against hope, they realised their goal lay not on the Barrier, but high upon the polar plateau. To reach it they must climb a huge glacier which, in their marching, they would find to measure 120 miles long and up to 30 miles wide, its sides sometimes enclosed within sheer granite walls rising to 2000 feet. Shackleton gave it the name of 'Beardmore' after the Scottish businessman who was his principal backer. He had found Antarctica's greatest known glacier and in the evidence of these immense mountains, some banded with deposits of coal and fossilised wood, additional confirmation that Antarctica was indeed more continental in nature.* His expedition had climbed Mount Erebus and he was confident of the South Magnetic Pole; now onwards to the ultimate prize, the Geographic South Pole.

The Southern Party had celebrated Christmas Day at an elevation of 9500 feet in 52 degrees of frost, with a double serve of hoosh and a cigar. Passage up the glacier was marked by blizzard, treacherous blue ice and untold crevasse falls and saves. 'We were killed a hundred times,' remembered Adams. When at last they reached the summit at 11,000 feet another 300 miles of man-hauling awaited on the bleak, featureless plateau. Shackleton suffered snow blindness and the drained food supply became critical, the largest daily meal reduced to three plasmon biscuits, a tablet of chocolate and a mug of cocoa. In the sub-zero temperatures of the plateau and 90-mile-per-hour winds, a shortage of breath brought on headaches and giddiness. For Shackleton the message was clear. In the British spirit of do-or-die, they could claim the Pole, but then it meant die.

---

* The Lambert Glacier in Australian Antarctic Territory, discovered in the 1950s, is the world's largest at 250 miles (400 km) long and averaging 25 miles (40 km) wide.

By 9 January they had been marching for 72 days and next to 730 miles. A few days more would have them the prize, but to tramp across the intervening 97 miles invited doom from starvation on the return. Shackleton gave the order to stop. 'We have shot our bolt.' He proclaimed possession of the plateau in the name of King Edward VII, took their photograph beside Queen Alexandra's flag, and buried a brass cylinder of postage stamps sent by the New Zealand Government. Then, at 88°23'S. they turned. His decision to protect himself and his comrades would have few equals in the annals of modern exploration. To Bertram, it was the most immense feat of courage, fortitude and self-denial. Shackleton saw much less heroics. In a letter to Emily, his wife, in characteristic breezy style he stated, 'I thought you'd rather have a live donkey than a dead lion'.*

---

* Shackleton's 'furthest south' became subject to the inevitable scrutiny of experts and antagonists. Some argued that he did not achieve his magic 'less than 100' miles from the Pole and more likely turned back at 88 degrees 16 minutes, suggesting a distance of 104 miles. For public consumption, 97 miles prevail.

CHAPTER 15

LAST DAYS

'We all turned out to give three cheers and take a last look at the place where we had spent so many happy days. The hut was not exactly a palatial residence . . . but it had been our home for a year and would always live in our memories.' The same hut that Shackleton farewelled still stands, a fragile matchbox affair cradled between a rocky ridge and the prominence of Cape Royds, and absurdly dwarfed against the mammoth white dome of a smoking volcano. Yet to the World Heritage Watch it is precious, a site where money must be spent to preserve those weathered planks and all the history they contain.

Once *Nimrod* got under way, no time could be spared to load the Northern Party's remaining samples stored on Depot Island. Knowing that a storm threatened, those left at the hut had to rush away, leaving Roberts' still warm bread half eaten on the plate.* A letter from the Prof tacked to the inner door 'for anyone who may

---

* From a visit to the deserted hut in 1912: 'It was very dark inside but I pulled the boarding down from the windows so that we could see all right. It was very funny to see everything lying about just as we had left it, in that last rush to get off in the lull of the blizzard. Nothing had been disturbed. On the table was the remains of a batch of bread that Bobs had cooked for us and that was only partially consumed before the *Nimrod* called for us. Some of the rolls showed the impression of bites given to them in 1909, all round the bread were the sauces, pickles, pepper and salt of our usual standing lunch, and a half-opened tin of gingerbreads

119

come' gave details of the expedition's work 'in case *Nimrod* is lost on the return voyage'. The thought of being trapped in McMurdo Sound, as *Discovery* had once been, was a risk no one wanted to run. 'We watched the little hut fade away in the distance,' Shackleton continued, 'with feelings almost of sadness and there were few men aboard who did not cherish a hope that some day they once more live strenuous days under the shadow of mighty Erebus.' They broke into a chorus of 'Old Lang Syne'.

The Boss reckoned he spoke for all his comrades as *Nimrod* churned through the pack and entered the Ross Sea. For him, comfort and, optimistically, fortune lay ahead in a secure and home-spun life from which he would promise Emily never to stray. Each of his men must have been filled with heady expectation of a hero's welcome, be it major or minor, when they reached whatever distant place they called home. David, Mawson, Murray and Priestly would complete the expedition's scientific reports* and, beyond that, return with heightened acclaim to their departments in academia; the sur-geons to demonstrate superior knowledge of practising medicine under the severest conditions of cold, trauma and discomfort; Murray to be acknowledged as a biologist of note for his observa-tions of their penguin neighbours and the microscopic rotifers of the freshwater lakes; Day to advertise his skills as first man to manage a motor car in Antarctica; Brocklehurst to return to his estate and lordly ways, and no doubt the darling of many a young lady; Marston to his studio, with reputation enhanced and in demand for

---

was witness to the dryness of the climate for they were still crisp as the day they were opened. The whole place is very eerie, there is such a feeling of life about it. Not only do I feel it but others do also. Last night after I turned in I could have sworn that I heard people shouting to each other. I thought that I had only got an attack of nerves but Campbell asked us if I had heard any shouting for he had certainly done so.' (Priestly in his *Antarctic Adventure*, 1914.)

* In their report, David and Priestly pay tribute to 'The valuable assistance rendered by our late colleague, Mr Bertram Armytage'. For Mawson, the seed had been planted to lead his own expedition, one wholly 'Australasian' in character.

his paintings of an awesome white continent; Adams with a deeper knowledge of polar weather and its influence on the world beyond; Wild, Joyce and Roberts to wonder where another adventure might take them.

Standing by *Nimrod*'s rail, watching phantom 'bergs slip through the mist, Bertram must have wondered about Shackleton's refusal to consider him for the Southern Party. That rejection belonged to the time of his mid-winter depression – hardly a recommendation for going to the Pole. Yet, as events unfolded, it was a decision that Shackleton might have regretted. Frank Wild, in his diary of the southern journey (held in the Scott Polar Research Institute, Cambridge) speaks of 'two grubscoffing useless beggars' who in his belief did not pull their weight as the four laboured up the Beardmore Glacier. He asked whether George Marston, young and husky, and another such as Ernest Joyce – who actually had been ruled medically unfit – could have made the difference to their faltering progress.

But what if that other place had been filled by 'a sterling fellow' . . . a man with no physical limitations and remembered as 'reliable . . . obedient . . . ready for any work'? Could a choice of the Australian have injected sufficient extra energy into the Southern Party to cover those remaining miles and get Britain to the Pole? Bertram might have wondered.

Enough said of dreams. Bertram needed now to contemplate what his world held in store. He was determined to make things different, to put down anchors, to contribute, to look for a profession or some other worthy occupation. He had had enough of being a chap whose career owned no fixed address. Money, property and friends were not his problem, nor was pride in physical fitness though he must admit that some of the old pursuits belonged to younger men. Besides there was a limit to how many lions, tigers, bears, elephants, kangaroo and deer a fellow could be expected to shoot. But shooting of a different style could be the key.

Before the expedition began, Bertram had considered submitting his name to the Imperial War Office for a post at the new Australian desk that was coming to grips with a young Commonwealth's desire for an independent defence force. The artillery, the South African War and the BAE were his credentials and he saw things as an Australian. Sir Edward Hutton, the fiery Major General who had moulded colonial defences when Bertram had served as a young officer at Fort Queenscliff, would certainly write in his support. Once they were in London Bertram would act! London also meant a reunion with Blanch, the wife of this part-time husband, and a daughter who had known her father no more than half of her tender four years. A letter brought down on *Nimrod* told him they were no longer living at Wooloomanata. Why? Emotions about his marriage were again brought to the surface and what the future held for them, as did his wonderings; what was the attraction of London for Blanch?

Across a Southern Ocean less stormy than on their outward voyage, and on a vessel less overburdened, Shackleton and his men reached Stewart Island and the southernmost New Zealand telegraph station on 22 March. From an anchorage in Half Moon Bay, Shackleton went ashore to a specially stationed morse-code operator waiting to send his message to the *Daily Mail* in London; no one else was allowed into town and no one from the island could come aboard. By the time of disembarking at Port Lyttelton two days later, the world knew of Shackleton's exploits. All of Christchurch seemed to stream down to view a battered *Nimrod* and shake hands with The Boss and his gallant company. Bertram and Brocklehurst were available to accompany him in public appearances that extended from the South Island to the North until finally on 14 April the government gave the official farewell lunch at the Grand Hotel in Wellington. In his speech, Shackleton promised that New Zealand would be well remembered when he exercised his privilege of naming their Antarctic discoveries: few men in modern times could match such an offer. When they sailed for Sydney on the *Riverina* next day, the prime minister, Sir Joseph Ward, was at the wharf to wave goodbye while students from Victoria College gave the full Maori hakka.

New Zealand's enthusiasm for a great explorer would be repeated across the Tasman Sea, starting in Sydney where a Lord Mayoral welcome drew the largest attendance of a lantern lecture in the Town Hall. To a delighted audience, Shackleton's inimitable humorous and conversational style brought a hitherto remote Antarctica alive with stories of penguins, icebergs, volcano and glaciers – all from the voice of a man who had actually lived through the icy perils. At a second lecture the governor general, Lord Dudley, called for three cheers for the expedition and its leader. But as the *Sydney Morning Herald* reminded, Shackleton had not reached Sydney to 'break' the expedition's story, for this had been ably done by Professor Edgeworth David who had arrived home three weeks earlier to be met with a huge reception that overflowed the Great Hall of Sydney University.*

After a similar reception in Melbourne where Bertram was reunited with his family, and especially with his cousin Leila and her sisters at Como, leaving with them his much-prized sledge, they moved on for another public welcome in Adelaide where Mawson was the local hero. On 13 May they sailed from Port Adelaide aboard RMS *India* bound for Port Said where a change would be made to the mail steamer *Isis* for a voyage across the Mediterranean to Italy and thence by express train to England. Shackleton spent much of the voyage working on his book with the New Zealand journalist Edward Saunders, formerly of the *Lyttelton Times*, who had been engaged to ensure the publisher's deadline would be met.

---

* *Nimrod* followed Shackleton from New Zealand to Sydney captained by J. K. Davis, then aged 25. Crowds visited the ship at Neutral Bay, examining the expedition's gear and looking for souvenirs. Seamen were reported to have done a profitable trade in selling 'Antarctic rock' taken from a nearby heap of Kiama basalt.

A young woman passenger recalled 'a Mr Armytage' being with
Shackleton as he played games with the children, yarned with the
ship's company and energetically paced the deck.

She described Shackleton's table in the dining saloon 'in constant
uproar' from his Irish wit and inexhaustible supply of funny stories,
so much so that the stewards' attempts at serving the guests frequently lapsed into giggles and spilt soup. At Brindisi where they left
the ship, Bertram farewelled his quasi-namesake Albert Armitage,
now master of the *Isis*. As Scott's second-in-command, Armitage had
engaged Shackleton for the Discovery expedition eight years before.
He had been first to climb the Ferrar Glacier and to reach the Polar
Plateau and his own name marked the southern tip of Ross Island,
which no one would forget.

In London, Shackleton and Emily were residents of the St James
Club, not too distant from the expedition's office at 9 Regent Street,
Waterloo Place, where Alfred Reid waited with a file of engage-
ments, accounts and correspondence that was designed to bring a
most-exalted explorer firmly down to earth. Bertram returned to his
usual digs at the Cavalry Club while the rest of the expedition,
ordered to be 'on station' for public appearances, returned to their
homes or, if too distant from London, stayed with Priestly who
offered a free bed at his house in Tewkesbury. Blanch Armytage and
daughter Mary were lodged at Ockley, a village in Surrey, and
whether or how often Bertram made the hour's train journey to be
with them we do not know; someone might ask whether it was an
odd separation considering Bertram had been absent for 18 months.

The return of the expedition to the public spotlight had actually
begun at Dover on 12 June where a mayoral welcome and a clamouring press awaited at the dock, and a cheering crowd heard
Shackleton unceremoniously introduce each of his men by their
Cape Royds nickname, presumably summoning Bertram to the
rostrum with the call of 'What!What!' Another wildly cheering
crowd saw Shackleton and Emily and their children ride through
London from Charring Cross Station in an open horse carriage.

As their universities were disinclined to give David and Mawson further leave, or to pay their overseas expenses, Bertram remained the sole Australian expeditionary in the weeks that followed of dining at the best hotels and the classiest private clubs. Priestly's diary records 'we were the lions of the London season' and instances a dinner in Park Lane given by Mr Eckstein, of the De Beers Company. 'On each plate was a model of *Nimrod* in white heather. The floral decorations alone would have kept us in clover for months . . . we were entertained by famous artists such as Clara Butt and soprano Tetrazzini . . . who would have cost £2000. What would we have not given for the equivalent in cash?' Yet after some of the evening's lavish entertainments they strolled home along the Embankment and, recalling the Barrier's chill, left money at the pie stalls for 'the stranded' dossing on the benches.

Fame and festivities reached a peak by mid June when two official events drew royalty and the elite of England in honouring Shackleton and his comrades. 'It is impossible to believe in the alleged degeneration of the British race,' said the chairman, Lord Halsbury FRS, after The Boss told his story to a luncheon of the Royal Societies Club of London. Indeed, Halsbury's remarks held the kernel of why this former lieutenant of the merchant marine and his odd-bod company were worth the fuss; against a world growing uncertain in the shadow of German militarism, Russian revolutionaries and a republic proclaimed in China, Britain needed the opportunity to make a statement that Britannia still ruled. The BAE which had flown the flag across Antarctica gave the same 'B' a chance to flex the Empire's muscles, especially after the unhappy experience of the South African War. So in the cause of patriotism let Sir Arthur Conan Doyle, the creator of Sherlock Holmes, propose a hearty vote of thanks, and give the seconding to Captain Robert Falcon Scott RN, who must quietly relish the prospect that the Pole could yet be his trophy. The same evening those of his men still in London came with Shackleton as guests of the publisher William Heinemann at the Savoy Hotel, followed by 'a cinematograph display illustrating the expedition'. The Boss gave a running commentary to the film, never neglecting to name the achievements of his men. The scenes they watched, he said, 'bear testimony to the single hearted devotions of my companions'.

The grand climax came on Monday 29 June at the Empress Room of the Royal Palace Hotel in Kensington where the Royal Geographical Society held a dinner prior to the presentation of its medals. Guests adjourned afterwards to the Albert Hall and another procession of nobility in a setting described in *The Times* as 'brilliant in the extreme, every division of the building being crowded with ladies in evening dress and gentlemen who wore distinguished orders . . .' Flanking the Prince and Princess of Wales sat the Italian ambassador, a Swedish minister and a host of admirals, archbishops, generals and knights of the realm, and others notable of politics and professions. After a screening, Shackleton, yet again, was invited to 'give an account of the results of the expedition, illustrated with lantern slides'. As *The Times* reported,

> Mr Shackleton was received with great cheering when he stepped forward to give his lecture. He spoke easily and clearly, and he was heard distinctly all over the hall. His humorous descriptions of wild life were keenly appreciated. The lantern slides were excellent – more particularly those of Mount Erebus in eruption . . . great cheering when again the lantern showed the Union Jack first at the Magnetic Pole and secondly at the extreme point of Mr Shackleton's expedition.

After Captain Scott and Admiral Sir Lewis Beaumont had disposed of the vote of thanks, the Prince of Wales came forward to present the Society's medal. For The Boss, it was in gold, emblazoned with the explorer's portrait. 'As a brother sailor I am proud to hand him this medal,' said the prince to Shackleton. From the royal hand, in recognition of their services, the other 12 who were able to be present received the same medal, but in silver and smaller. Bertram got his.

More glory lay ahead. Shackleton was made a Commander of the Royal Victorian Order, as Scott had been before him, and on 9 November, the same day that his book was launched, his name appeared in the King's birthday honours list of knighthoods (which so far had eluded Captain Scott). Alongside Sir Ernest Shackleton and his old Shore Party comrades, Bertram stood to attention at Buckingham Palace on 14 December to have King Edward VII pin the silver Polar Medal on his breast. Antarctica's highest award was his. He stood there for Australia. Could a man wish for any greater recognition?

The letter from the War Office, delivered to the Cavalry Club, politely declined his application for a post at the new Australian desk. His service record was not in question, it was his age. He was too old to fit into the structured promotions ladder. He was too old. For months he had been waiting in London, hoping. Seeing his chums fit back into their slots. Reading *The Heart of the Antarctic*, published in two volumes after just five months in preparation and now a bestseller in the bookshops. Applauding the government's decision to grant Shackleton £20,000. Hearing that Mawson was raising an Australasian Antarctic expedition which Wild would join, while Priestly and Day had agreed to go with Scott in his new attempt to reach the Pole. Everybody fitting back into their slots; everyone with a purpose to fulfil, but him. Dispiriting, what-what?

By late 1909, Shackleton's circus has lost its zing. Bertram arrived back in Australia at the end of January. He returned to Wooloomanata to see his parents and brothers, visited his cousins at Como and friends in Toorak and was seen sometimes at the Club, but more often stopped at Menzies Hotel which was his favoured city address. Early in March he caught the train to Sydney, knowing that he might find two comrades who could offer him counsel. While waiting at the Hotel Australia he met Leo Cotton, the young man from David's staff who had come south on *Nimrod*'s first voyage and then returned. They had a long and pleasant talk about old times, according to Cotton, who advised that the Professor and

Priestly were away in Queensland, giving fundraising lectures for the
expedition's delayed scientific memoir. At once Bertram knew that
his telegram to the University of Sydney would not have been
received. He abruptly booked out of the hotel and caught the night
train to Melbourne.

In Melbourne Bertram visited the family solicitors, Blake and
Riggall in William Street, and on 8 March signed his will; yet
nothing in his action suggested the foreboding. He booked in at
Menzies, stayed two nights, and then with bags packed advised he
was transferring to the Club. Albert Smith, the hotel porter, carried
the three portmanteaux to the cab, and saluted farewell. Smith:
'He was always a lonely sort of man; but there was a queer, miserable
look in his eyes the last few days. When he left the hotel on Saturday
afternoon, he seemed cheerful enough then. He was going to stay at
the Melbourne Club, and he gave me a tip, and said goodbye in the
heartiest way. No one would guess that there was anything serious
the matter. He used to go out cycling by himself a good deal, and,
now I think of it, it did seem as though there was something preying
on his mind that he was trying to shake off.'

At the Melbourne Club, William Dixon, the assistant valet, carried
the luggage upstairs to room 24 and just before six o'clock delivered
a jug of hot water. He was the last person to see Bertram alive.

A PECULIAR CHAP

We were awfully upset here about poor old Armytage's sad death. We raised several hundred pounds as a result of our tour and returned to Sydney, just in time to miss an S.O.S. from Bertram, who was obviously in mental distress. I rushed to the Hotel Australia to find he had that day returned to Melbourne. On the Monday we read in the papers that he had dressed himself in his evening clothes with all his medals, laid down on the floor of his room in the Melbourne Club on a carefully spread mackintosh, and blown his brains out. We can neither of us get rid of the feeling that if we had seen him we could probably have saved him. Had we been at home when his message arrived, we could doubtless have pointed him out some way in which he could do useful exploring even in a small way, given him hope and provided him with an objective, his two great needs. He was plainly oppressed by the idea that he was no use in the world. He was a peculiar chap, very introspective, but one of the best.

[Priestly, in a letter to Brocklehurst]

CHAPTER 16

WHY?

'I find that on March 12, at the Melbourne Club, Bertram Armytage died from a gunshot wound in the head, wilfully self-inflicted, with a Colt automatic pistol. There is not sufficient evidence to determine the state of his mind at the time.'

The coroner's verdict, handed down at the Melbourne morgue on 17 March, brought to a close a week of shock at the news of Bertram's suicide. Professor Edgeworth David hastened to mail a copy of the *Sydney Morning Herald* report to Alfred Reid, manager of the BAE office in London. 'In him we have undoubtedly lost a simple minded, gallant and loyal friend', David wrote from his rooms at the University of Sydney. 'I am sure that Sir Ernest [Shackleton] and other members of the expedition will feel his loss very much.' Of their old sledging companion, he concluded with a reflection. 'He was a man who did not know what fear was, but was of a very sensitive disposition. He was accustomed to be alone a good deal, and I presume his nerve balance was upset by too much introspecting and brooding over a number of small disappointments and worries.'

Shackleton, soon to begin a hero's lecture tour of Europe and the United States, sent a message of condolence from London that was widely reported in the Australian press, 'Mr Armytage was a loyal and zealous member of the expedition, good for any emergency, and always ready to work'. Shackleton also wrote a personal letter to Blanch but the contents, unfortunately, are among the lost Armytage papers.

In his letter to Philip Brocklehurst, now returned to his Staffordshire estate, Priestly spoke of the 'mental distress' of the man who had led them in the Western Party. 'He was a peculiar chap, very introspective, but one of the best.' Climbing the Ferrar Glacier with Bertram must have been a memory that loomed large in both these young explorers' minds.

At three o'clock on Friday afternoon, 15 March, Bertram's private funeral, yet attended by many from the Melbourne Club, went from Como to the Boroondara Cemetery. Bertram's father and two of his brothers, Frank and Frederick, were the chief mourners, while the pallbearers included George Chirnside, two relatives from his mother's Staughton family, Club president and racehorse owner A. D. Murphy, and Robert Cornish, secretary of the Melbourne Club. In those times, because of the suicide, a church burial was not held to be appropriate and, instead, graveside prayers in the Church of England tradition were offered by the Reverend T. H. Rust, an Armytage relative.

As the coffin was lowered into the soil of suburban Kew, Robert Cornish may have watched with an extra insight into Bertram's troubled mind. The coroner, Dr Cole, noted in his finding the letter written by Bertram to Cornish, his friend. After reading the contents he agreed it seemed to show that suicide was contemplated. As the Melbourne press reported in an extract from the coroner's report:

> The letter referred incidentally to his disappointment in not obtaining a position he sought at the Imperial War Office. That probably played on his mind, and upset his mental balance, till he gave way to a sudden impulse. There was no doubt about it being a case of suicide – and suicide in the prime of life when he had everything to make life desirable, youth, wealth, health and a host of friends, except one thing, and the want of that must have driven to self-murder.

In recording his verdict Dr Cole said that for sentimental reasons Mr Cornish desired that the letter he received from Mr Armytage should not be published.

In an age when sea travel was the only option between England and Australia, Blanch obviously could not attend her husband's funeral. Two months, in fact, elapsed before we find evidence of her reaction to Bertram's death. On 8 May from her accommodation at Hill Side in Ockley village, Surrey, she wrote to Mr Reid at the BAE office in London:

> I should like you know, and any of the others who feel interested in my husband, that I have received all there is to get from Australia, to explain why he took his life from us. There is no reason known; it was hoped he had left a letter for me, and I was cabled to wait till the mail came; it has come and gone; he said goodbye to no one. So there is nothing to know.
>
> They all write me that they feel he had no intention of doing what he did up to the last. He wrote me most cheerfully to the last, the letter dated 8 March only three days before he took his life – every thing was well.
>
> I have not written Sir Ernest Shackleton. I should be glad if you would let him know I have no news – no reason to give him.
>
> I should be so glad to know where Mr Wild is and where an address would find him. I do not leave for Australia, where I must go to see to matters of my husband, till September.
>
> Believe me, yours very sincerely,
>
> [signed] Blanch Armytage

POSTSCRIPT

On 30 November 1910 the Supreme Court of Victoria granted probate to the will of the late Bertram Armytage which amounted to an estate of £12,291.10.0 in realisable cash and other assets. The will gave £5000 to Blanch 'for her own absolute use' together with interest earned on the remainder of the estate which was then to be awarded to Mary, their daughter, on her attaining the age of 21 years, or earlier upon marriage. If neither wife nor daughter survived, the beneficiary would be the University of Melbourne. Two years later his father Frederick William of Wooloomanata died at Como, but this was an inheritance he would never claim, instead it went to the woman who remained Bertram's widow for another 45 years.*

Bertram's suicide was not the only tragedy that awaited the BAE members who shared the hut at Cape Royds. James Murray and Forbes Mackay joined Vilhjalmur Stefansson's Canadian Arctic Expedition and both were lost in February 1914 when making a bid

---

* 'Armytage. On May 16, 1955, Blanch Dunn, widow of Bertram Armytage, late of *Wooloomanata*, Lara. Loved mother of Mary Staughton Armytage-Macdonald, of Kenya. Aged 84 years.' (A death notice in Melbourne newspapers of 17 May 1955.)

for safety after their ship, *Karluk*, sank in the ice of the Chukchi Sea off the coast of Siberia.

Tragedy of a different kind overtook Frank Wild, the most seasoned of all the old Antarctic hands, and a friend of Bertram's. He joined Mawson's 1911–1914 Australasian expedition and then served as second-in-command of Shackleton's ill-fated Imperial Trans-Antarctic Expedition of 1914–1916, and again went with Shackleton in 1921. After retiring to South Africa, he failed as a cotton farmer in Natal, took to drink and died in 1939, spending his last years as a penniless rouseabout.

Of Bertram's fellow Australians in the BAE, Mawson would lead two more Antarctic ventures and on the first, his Australasian expedition of 1911, came close to losing his own life after the deaths of his two sledging companions, Belgrave Ninnis and Xavier Mertz, far from the base at Commonwealth Bay. His last expedition was in the summer of 1929–1930 and 1930–1931, on *Discovery*. As Professor of Geology at the University of Adelaide, Sir Douglas Mawson played an important role in Australia's polar planning until his death in 1958 at the age of 76.

While in his mid 50s, the indefatigable Professor Edgeworth David, in a break from writing the BAE's scientific reports, enlisted in the Australian Imperial Force and with the rank of major advised tunnel diggers who were driving against German trenches on the Western Front. As Professor of Geology at the University of Sydney, David was regarded as 'the father of Australian geological science'. Like his once-pupil Mawson, he received a knighthood and a state funeral upon his death in Sydney in 1934. Leo Cotton, the young student who sailed on *Nimrod*, was David's successor in the Chair of Geology.

Peaceful old age finally claimed Bertram's two sledging companions of the Western Party which he led on the Ferrar Glacier. Raymond Priestly, after serving in Scott's 1910–1912 expedition, survived World War One, winning a Military Cross, and afterwards, with Frank Debenham (the Australian-born geologist of the second Scott expedition) was influential in founding the Scott Polar Research Institute at the University of Cambridge. In 1934 he became the first salaried vice-chancellor at the University of Melbourne and in 1938 vice-chancellor of the University of Birmingham, where he was knighted in 1952. His Antarctic connection continued with an acting directorship of the Falkland Islands Dependencies Survey (now the British Antarctic Survey) and a presidency of the Royal Geographical Society. He died in 1974, aged 87.

Sir Philip Brocklehurst, whose prickly attitude towards Bertram is recorded, had Shackleton as best man when he wed a few years after returning from Cape Royds. He saw active duty in both world wars and, as last survivor of the BAE's Shore Party, died at his Staffordshire estate of Swythamley Park in 1975, aged 88.

John King Davis, though not a member of the Shore Party, is the superb master mariner who was *Nimrod*'s first officer and later captain on its return to Australia. He captained *Aurora* in Mawson's 1911–1914 expedition and, with *Aurora*, returned to Antarctica to retrieve the marooned Ross Sea party of Shackleton's *Endurance* expedition. Later he was master of *Discovery* in Mawson's BANZARE* first voyage of 1929–1930 (there was a second voyage, 1930–1931). He became Commonwealth Director of Navigation in 1920, retired in 1949, and died in Melbourne, aged 83, in 1967.

They all outlived the dynamic leader who took them on a great Antarctic adventure and brought them safely home. The Boss, aged 48, died of a heart attack aboard his ship, *Quest*, on 5 January 1922 while once again heading towards the white magnet of the south that had consumed his life. Sir Ernest Shackleton's grave is located at Grytviken on the remote sub-Antarctic island of South Georgia.

As for Bertram's surviving earthly treasures, his sledge is kept by Melbourne Museum and sometimes placed on display, his medals in

---

* The British, Australian and New Zealand Antarctic Research Expedition of 1929–1931, which also led to the claiming of Australian Antarctic Territory.

the wall cabinet at Como are for all to see, while the polar collection of the Royal Geographical Society in London claims a belt, knife and pocket knife; within the family, Rex Armytage holds a mirror by which Bertram is believed to have heliographed the searching *Nimrod* in McMurdo Sound.

The depressive moods noted in Bertram no doubt could have been treated with medication in a more modern age; for his part Bertram, in the pride of his physical prowess, does not present as a man who would have sought the doctor. Yet one legacy of his life remains in the annual Bertram Armytage Prize for Medicine or Surgery at the University of Melbourne which his mother established with a grant of £500 in 1920. One wonders if a recipient of the prize knows anything of the man in whose name it is given. Bertram's taking of his own life was tragedy enough, but perhaps his exclusion from the Southern Party was tragedy of a different kind; the conquest of the South Pole could have been a much different story.

Within two days of Bertram's death, the possibility that the rejection by the War Office for a post in London as a factor in his suicide was widely circulated in the press. One has to ask if this convenient story was reason enough for the man to put a gun to his head. The fact that he returned alone to Australia from London did not escape comment. Blanch, upon news of her husband's death, says in a letter that she and their infant daughter do not plan to return to Melbourne for another seven months. Evidence of their relationship points to several years of a dysfunctional marriage. No mention of 'loving', be it husband or wife, appears on the austere headstone which she placed on his grave. Nothing said about the expedition. He was already a forgotten Antarctic man.

Perhaps Blanch was a wife fed up with moods and career soul-searching. For his part, in the perambulations from Boer War to BAE, and what else in between, Bertram does not appear to want the role of a comforting and satisfying husband. But the society in which they mixed had moved from the closet tone of the 'naughty nineties' to Edwardian complicity, in the style of the monarch himself, with a degree of licentiousness in which affairs, by man or woman, were accepted – with due discretion.

The element of mystery surrounding Bertram's married life remains inseparable from his time in Antarctica. Blanch says that she received a cheerful letter from her husband written but three days before his death. Clearly in his will, Bertram does nothing to penalise his wife. Yet rumours persist that, during his absence, Blanch was involved in an affair in London with a member of the old squattocracy who had been among Bertram's best friends. Whether such a factor, if correct, would have been sufficient amid a trough of despondency to push him to self-destruction is a matter for contemplation. David wrote about 'too much introspection and brooding'. The same introspection could help to explain the deliberate theatre of putting on the dress suit, placing the medals on show, spreading the counterpane and settling pillows beneath the head before pulling the trigger. Some family members have a more succinct postscript to Bertram's tragic end: 'The wrong man got the bullet.'

APPENDIX

1. PRESS INTERVIEW WITH ARMYTAGE

Sydney Morning Herald, 6 April 1909
The Antarctic Expedition
Lieutenant Shackleton's Tactfulness
Mr. Armytage's Appreciation.

Melbourne. Monday. Mr. Armytage, who accompanied Lieutenant Shackleton in his famous expedition in Antarctica in the course of an interview today said: Life on the depot in the hut was very pleasant. I put on a lot of weight. We lived like fighting cocks because, of course, we had to get well and fit for the hardships and trials which were expected in the spring. We never had time on our hands. There was always mending and sewing to be done and besides there was a good deal of work about the hut. A penguin rookery was useful to us. The birds were there when we first arrived. We went in amongst them and killed about a hundred of them. We did not shoot them. It was mere slaughter. They had absolutely no fear of men. They did not know what man was, and let us walk right in among them and knock them over. Even after we had killed as many they still betrayed no fear. We did not pluck or dress the birds. We just flung them on the roof of the hut. There they became frozen hard – a natural refrigerating chamber. When we wanted to use one, we went to the larder on the roof, took the bird inside, thawed it out and prepared it for cooking. They made very good eating indeed, and were a welcome addition to our provisions. We also drew largely on the penguin rookery for eggs. The eggs are very large with small yolks and large whites. They were very nice to eat.

The effect of the sun on the snow and ice was most dazzling. We all wore goggles. Large motor goggles were tried, but we found that smaller goggles ventilated at the side were cooler and better. We had orange-tinted glasses. In that way we were saved from snow blindness. The four ponies which remained to us at the end of the winter all went blind. I believe, from snow blindness. Of course they did not seem to be affected by cold. None of them suffered from frost bite. Even their feet were not affected. A great change came over their coats during the winter. They were always shaggy, but their coats became woolly and thick like the woolly pelted horse of Neolithic times that Kipling wrote about. They were all in excellent condition at the end of the winter.

From my point of view the expedition was most interesting. But of course I am a sportsman, and there is no life down there except the seals and penguins, and they do not provide sport. In the north polar region there is an abundance of game. Nevertheless seals are very useful. Professor David and his party [to the South Magnetic Pole] were forced to live upon them when their provisions became exhausted. To scientists, however, Antarctica is an inexhaustible field. All through from first to the last the scientists in the expedition never lacked for new discoveries of enthralling interest.

The success of the expedition is due mainly to Lieutenant Shackleton. He is an ideal leader. In the first place, he is a wonderful organizer. The whole of the expedition, down to the trivial details, had been carefully thought out beforehand. The organization was perfect. Everything that was needed was provided. Then, Lieutenant Shackleton was able to handle the men well. He knows how to keep them in good heart, and has a rare charm of manner and a wonderful memory. He forgets nothing that he has seen or heard. We saw a great deal of him and learned to appreciate fully his splendid abilities as a leader of men. We would be perhaps a little morose and gloomy, and Lieutenant Shackleton would see it. In about 10 minutes he would have everybody laughing and happy again.

The expedition is not disbanded. We are still Shackleton's men. We are to meet in England in June, and then, after everything has been finally discussed and disposed of, we shall be disbanded. Of course there is still a great deal to be done in the final working out of results and the finishing off of the work begun down south. Only second to Lieutenant Shackleton's leadership were the remarkable skill and courage and tact displayed by Professor David. His pluck and energy were wonderful, but they are amply shown by the work he accomplished.

2. SHACKLETON'S INSTRUCTIONS TO ARMYTAGE

BRITISH ANTARCTIC EXPEDITION 1907

Oct 28th 1908
Cape Royds
Antarctica

Dear Sir:

You will follow the instructions contained in the following letter.

You are to take command of a sledge party consisting of Brocklehurst Priestly and yourself to carry out geological and other explorations in the Western Mountains leaving Cape Royds about the 1st of December, 1908.

1. The exact date of your departure will be given you by the officer in charge of the Expedition at that time. I am unable to fix the actual date of your departure as I shall be absent and the ice conditions may have altered during November.

2. Your party is to be fully equipped and provisioned for five weeks and this is to be done at Cape Royds.

3. If the ice conditions are favourable the motor will carry your party as far as possible towards towards pinnacle ice: if the motor cannot travel you are to steer for Glacier Tongue and from thence to the pinnacle ice then skirt the pinnacle ice and steer for Butter Point. You must not travel on the sea ice at a distance too far from fast ice to allow you to reach the latter in the event of the break up of the sea ice.

4. On reaching Butter Point you are to search for the depot which the Northern Party has arranged to leave there: on finding it you are to examine and carefully note the amount of provisions then cache all your provisions and oil except sufficient to carry you to Glacier Tongue where you will load up again and return to Butter Point. You are to load sufficient stores and oil at the Glacier to keep your party and the Northern Party in supplies. Your party is to be kept in supplies sufficient to last you until Jan 28th and the Northern Party in supplies from Jan 3rd to Jan 20th. You will calculate the amount of provisions and stores left by the Northern Party and by you on your first arrival at Butter Point. Load your sledge with the necessary amount of stores to enable these two parties to be kept in supplies to suit the above dates. If seals or birds are plentiful at Butter Point you can cut down the pemmican supply. You are to take west with you on your journey from Cape Royds the articles that the Northern Party left here.

5. You will then proceed to ascend the South Arm of the Ferrar Glacier directing your course upwards keeping on the north side of the Glacier until you pass the region of broken ice. After passing the area of disturbance you are to proceed to any locality that the geologist Priestly thinks most suitable for his work always having due regard for the safety of the party under your care.

6. The main object of your journey is geological exploration therefore you are to give every facility for the carrying out of this work.

7. I wish to have the most likely places for fossils examined at places of low altitude first before you proceed to higher altitude. The geologist will acquaint you with the likely places and if he can see nothing that is likely to prove interesting he will inform you and you will then proceed to a greater altitude. If fossils are found at any spot you are to camp there and load up as many specimens as possible. Bearing in mind my instruction contained in Par. 10 of this letter.

8. If it is necessary to proceed as high as Depot Nunatak you are to be specially careful as to your camping arrangements when passing through the area known as the North West Area, and particularly when in the vicinity of Windy Gully.

9 Should any member of your party show signs of mountain sickness you are to descend to a lower altitude.

10. You are to return to your depot at Butter Point reaching it not later than January the 7th 1909 and wait there keeping a lookout for the Northern Party. The Northern Party should arrive at Butter Point any time from the third of January 1909. When you meet the Northern Party you are to hand the enclosed instructions to Professor David. If Professor David has been lost during the Expedition of his Party, Mawson will be in command and the orders are to be handed to him. On the arrival of the Northern Party you will find in my instructions to Professor David the disposal of your party.

11. Should the Northern Party not arrive at Butter Point by the 25th of January you are to take your party to Glacier Tongue if the ice permits: if not you will proceed to Hut Point and keep a lookout for the 'Nimrod' from the vicinity of that spot. You can erect a flagstaff on the Point and rig a flag on it as a guide to the ship.

In the orders contained in this letter there is a certain amount of latitude allowed you except in the matter of your arrival and stay at Butter Point to await the Northern Party and in the instructions contained Pars 4 and 10. I trust to your discretion in all other matters feeling sure that you will successfully carry out the objects of the Journey. In addition to the geological work, Brocklehurst will carry on the photographic work and you will take charge of the meteorological observations. You will also keep a full record of your journey.

The journey you are to undertake is by no means an easy one and the complete fulfilment and objects will do much towards furthering the general success of the Expedition; therefore in selecting you to command this party I am placing a confidence in you that I consider justified after what I have seen of your work here and when as a member of the earliest sledge journey made in the Antarctic before the winter night was over, when you were with me on the above journey.

Wishing you good weather and good health
  I am Sir
  Yours faithfully
  Earnest H. Shackleton
  Commander B.A.E. 1907
B. Armytage Esq.
Cape Royds
Antarctica

3. ARMYTAGE'S REPORT TO SHACKLETON (CAPE ROYDS)

24–25 January 1909

When we found that the ice had gone out we struck camp, loaded up the sledge, and started away with the object of seeing whether we could get off the floe to the north. The position seemed to be rather serious, for we could not hope to cross any stretch of open water, there was no reasonable expectation of assistance from the ship, and most of our food was at Butter Point. We had not gone very far to the north before we came to an impassable lane of open water, and we decided to return to our original position. We went into camp and had breakfast at 11 am. Then we held a consultation and agreed that it would be best to stop where we then were for a time, at any rate, on the off-chance of the ship coming along one of the lanes to pick us up on the following day, or of the current changing and the ice once more touching the shore. We waited till three o'clock in the afternoon, but there did not seem to be any improvement in the position. The killer-whales were spouting in the channels, and occasionally bumping the ice under us. Then we marched north again, but met with open water in every direction, and after we had marched right round the floe we got into camp at the old position at 10 pm. We had a small meal of hoosh and biscuit. We had only four days' provisions on the floe with us, and I decided that we would have to go on short rations. We were encouraged by the fact that we had apparently ceased to move north, and were perhaps getting nearer the fast ice again. We got into our sleeping-bags in order to keep warm. At 11.30 pm Brocklehurst turned out to see whether the position had changed, and reported that we seemed to be within a few hundred yards of the fast ice, and still moving towards the land. I got out of my bag and put on my finnesko, and at midnight saw that we were very close to the fast ice, probably not more than two hundred yards away. I ran back as fast as I could, deciding that there was a prospect of an attempt to get ashore proving successful, and gave the other two men a shout. They struck the camp and loaded up within a very few minutes, while I went back to the edge of the floe at the spot towards which chance had first directed my steps. Just as the sledge got up to me, I felt the floe bump the fast ice. Not more than six feet of the edge touched, but we were just at that spot, and we rushed over the bridge thus formed. We had only just got over when the floe moved away again, and this time it went north to the open sea. The only place at which it touched the fast ice was that to which I had gone when I left the tent, and had I happened to go to any other spot we would not have escaped. We made our way to Butter Point, and at about three o'clock in the morning camped and had a good meal. Then we turned in and slept. When we got up for breakfast, there was open water where we had been drifting on the floe, and I sighted the *Nimrod* under sail, ten or twelve miles out. We laid the heliograph on to the vessel, and after flashing for about an hour got a reply. The *Nimrod* came alongside the fast ice at three o'clock in the afternoon of January 26, and we went on board with our equipment and specimens. We left a depot of provisions and oil at Butter Point in case the Northern Party should reach that point after our departure.

4. SHACKLETON DESCRIBES THE HUT

Shackleton described the immediate surroundings of the hut in *The Heart of the Antarctic*, 1909: 'From the door of our hut, which faced the north-west, we commanded a splendid view of the sound and the western mountains. On coming out of the door one had only to go round the corner of the building in order to catch a glimpse of Mount Erebus, which lay directly behind us. Its summit was about fifteen miles from our winter quarters, but its slopes and foothills commenced within three-quarters of a mile of the hut. Our view was cut off in all directions from the east to the south-east, where lay Cape Barne. To the right was Flagstaff Point, and to the left lay, at the head of the Bay, the slopes of Erebus.

'Our walks amongst the hills and across the frozen lakes were a great source of health and enjoyment and as a field of work for geologists and biologists, Cape Royds far surpassed Hut Point. The largest lake, which lay about half a mile to the north-east, was named Blue Lake, from the intensely vivid blue of the ice. This lake was peculiarly interesting to Mawson, who made the study of ice part of his work. Beyond Blue Lake, to the northward, lay Clear Lake, the deepest inland body of water in our vicinity. To the left as one looked north, close to the coast, was a circular basin which we called Coast Lake, where, when we first arrived, hundreds of skua gulls were bathing and flying about. Following the coast from this point back towards winter quarters was another body of water called Green Lake. In all these various lakes something of interest to science was discovered.'

Shackleton's description of the hut interior and surrounds continues: 'It was not a very spacious dwelling for the accommodation of fifteen persons, but our narrow quarters were warmer than if the hut had been larger. The coldest part of the house when we first lived in it was undoubtedly the floor, which was formed of inch tongue-and-groove boarding, but was not double-lined. There was a space of about four feet under the hut at the north-west end, the other end resting practically on the ground, and it was obvious to us that as long as this space remained we would suffer from the cold, so we decided to make an airlock of the area under the hut. To this end we decided to build a wall round the south-east and southerly sides, which were to windward, with the bulk of the provision cases. To make certain that no air would penetrate from these sides we built the first two or three tiers of cases a little distance out from the walls of the hut, pouring in volcanic earth until no gaps could be seen, and the earth was level with the cases; then the rest of the stores were piled up to a height of six or seven feet.

'On either side of the porch two other buildings were gradually erected. One, built out of biscuit cases, the roof covered with felt and canvas, was a store-room for Wild, who looked after the issue of all food-stuffs. The building on the other side of the porch was a much more ambitious affair, and was built by Mawson, to serve as a chemical and physical laboratory. It was destined, however, to be used solely as a store-room, for the temperature within its walls was practically the same as that of the outside air, and the warm, moist atmosphere rushing out from the hut covered everything inside this store-room with fantastic ice crystals.

'The lee side of the hut ultimately became the wall of the stables, for we decided to keep the ponies sheltered during the winter. The dog kennels were placed close to the porch of the hut, but only three of the dogs were kept constantly chained up. The meteorological station was on the weather side of the hut on the top of a small ridge, about twenty feet above the hut and forty feet above sea-level, and a natural path led to it. As readings of the instruments were to be taken day and night at intervals of two hours, and as it was quite possible that the weather might be so thick that a person might be lost in making his way between the screen and the hut, a line was rigged up on posts which were cemented into the ground by ice, so that in the thickest weather the observer could be sure of finding his way by following this very substantial clue.'

5. SHACKLETON PENGUIN SKETCH

This fragile chalk drawing of a penguin was sketched by Sir Ernest Shackleton in 1909 to illustrate public lectures given on his return, in that year, from the Antarctic. The blackboard was found lying in the basement of the Scott Polar Research Institute, having been in storage since 1998.

6. DEATH OF ARMYTAGE

The Argus, Melbourne, Monday, 14 March 1910

CAREER CUT SHORT.

SOLDIER AND EXPLORER.

BERTRAM ARMYTAGE SHOOTS HIMSELF.

Mr. Bertram Armytage, well known as a member of the Shackleton Antarctic Exhibition, and a popular clubman in Melbourne and London, shot himself in his bedroom at the Melbourne Club at 20 minutes past 6 o'clock on Saturday evening. The affair was deliberately planned, though the motive which seems to have prompted it was of no great importance.

It is only about six weeks since Mr. Armytage returned to Australia from London, where the members of the Shackleton party had met to bring together the threads of the expedition. He was staying at Menzies' Hotel, except during occasional absences in Sydney. Always a somewhat moody man, he betrayed no unusual signs of depression or mental trouble. He entertained his friends there in the ordinary way, though the servants noticed that at times he paced about the hotel in a lonely, hopeless fashion.

"He always used to do that," said one of the hotel attendants yesterday. "He was always a lonely sort of man; but there was a queer, miserable look in his eyes the last few days. He left the hotel on Saturday afternoon, and seemed cheerful enough then. He was going to stay at the Melbourne Club, and he gave me a tip, and said good-bye in the heartiest way. No one would guess that there was anything serious the matter. He used to go out cycling by himself a good deal, and, now I think of it, it did seem as though there was something preying on his mind that he was trying to shake off."

After leaving the hotel on Saturday, he

ACKNOWLEDGEMENTS AND SOURCES

Many people have joined in researching Bertram's story and assisting me to trace his footsteps. In particular I would like to thank the three Js, Jess Brown in the UK, and Janice Kesterton and Jean Whelan in Melbourne who, at the author's request, undertook detailed and often demanding detective work; and my wife Catherine – ever at my right hand with the computer; and Liz Anya-Petrivna of the National Trust, Victoria, who opened the doors to Como. Sincere thanks for their contribution are also offered to Peter Alsop, Michael Bryden, Dale Budd, Anne, Jane and Margaret Burke, Michael Collins Persse, David Cowdrey, Jonothan Davis, Paddy Elworthy, Jim Harvey, Beth Hechle, Bob Marmion, Stephen Martin, Nicola McColl, Mark Pharaoh, Neil Robertson, Bruce Rosenberg, Justin Smith, Carleen Watson; and staff of the Australian Antarctic Division, the La Trobe Library, University of Melbourne Archives, Mitchell Library, National Library, the Royal Historical Society of Victoria, the South Australian Museum, the Scott Polar Research Institute; and the memories of many old Antarctic hands.

The quotations attributed to Sir Ernest Shackleton are taken from his book, *The Heart of the Antarctic*, published in London by William Heinemann, 1909. Other extracts are from BAE diaries of Marshall, Priestly and Wild held by the Scott Polar Research

Institute, University of Cambridge. Images are mainly taken from the collections of the Watson family, the National Trust at Como, the albums of A. W. Allen, held in the Mitchell Library (State Library of New South Wales), the State Library of Victoria, University of Melbourne Archives and the author's own files. For sharing his insights into the life and times of the Armytage family, the author records his gratitude to Bertram's grand nephew, Rex Armytage, of Colac, Victoria.

In reconstructing the elusive life of Bertram Armytage, valuable discussions were also held with Mark Pharaoh (South Australian Museum), Carleen Watson (Watson and Chirnside families) and Herb Dartnall (BAE science). Information was sought from the Australian Government Antarctic Division, Hobart and the Polar Collections of the South Australian Museum, Adelaide, and La Trobe Library, Melbourne. Other contacts were made with National Archives, Canberra, the Geelong Historical Society and Geelong Grammar School, Melbourne Museum, University of Melbourne Archives, the Royal Historical Society of Victoria and Mitchell Library, Sydney. Information gained from overseas sources included communication with Jesus College Archives, Cambridge, The Cavalry and Guards Club, London, The Royal Scots Dragoons Guards secretariat, Edinburgh Castle. Polar history has been drawn from a wide spectrum of Antarctic literature, commencing with Shackleton's classic *The Heart of the Antarctic*. From the treasury of Antarctic literature was also drawn the backgrounds in F. and E. Jacka's *Mawson's Antarctic Diaries*, Scott's *The Voyage of the Discovery*, M. and J. Fisher's *Shackleton*, J. K.Davis's *High Latitude* and Molly David's *Professor David: The Life of Sir Edgeworth David*. More recent publications of great value have been R. E. Huntford's *Shackleton*, Beau Riffenburg's *Nimrod*, David Branagan's *T. W. Edgeworth David: A Life* and Tom Griffith's *Slicing the Silence*.

VICTORIA AND MELBOURNE SOCIETY

Chapter 1: The location of Mount Armytage ('a dome-shaped mountain north of the Mawson Glacier in Victoria Land') is noted in the *Antarctic Gazetteer*, SCAR ref. 527. Allowing for the interruption of a weekend, the news of Bertram Armytage's suicide first appeared in Melbourne newspapers and those of other capital cities on Monday morning, 14 March. The story of the Melbourne Club is told in R. McNicoll's *No. 96 Collins Street*. Como is dealt with in various National Trust of Victoria publications and in A. Selzer's *The Armytages of Como*; University of Melbourne archives hold extensive records and photographs of the house and family. Chapter 2: The Geelong Historical Society has recorded the histories of Elcho and Wooloomanata which also appear in Ian Wynd's *So Fine a Country: A History of the Shire of Corio*. The age of squattocracy is covered in N. Chapman's *Historic Homes of Western Victoria* and a detailed study of the Armytages is to be found in A. Henderson's *Early Pioneer Families of Victoria and the Riverina*; Armytage and Chirnside are significant entries in the Australian Dictionary of Biography 1851–1890; a list of Armytage pupils appears in J. Cornfield and M. Persse's *Geelong Grammarians: A Biographical Register 1855–1913*. Chapter 3: Correspondence with Dr J. Wilmoth, Jesus College archivist, provided some detail of university life during Bertram's attendance at Cambridge. *Liber Melburniensis* lists pupils of Melbourne Grammar School; from Geelong Historical Society records, and R. Marmion, Fort historian, information was obtained on the workings of Fort Queenscliff from the 1800s. L. C. Cox's *The Galloping Guns of Rupertswood and Werribee Park* tells the story of Victoria's mounted artillery while other sources are W. Billett's *Victoria's Guns* and R. Nicholls' *The Colonial Volunteers*. Chapter 4: Chirnside family history is accessible through a variety of records at the Royal Victorian Historical Society while a particular study is A. Ronald's *Wool Past the Winning Post: The Chirnside Family*. P. de Serville's *Pounds and Pedigrees: Upper Class Victoria 1850–1880* documents the gold- and wool-rich colony's early social history, with later years discussed in M. Cannon's series on Victorian life concluding with *The Long Last Summer*. Information on the Watson family is held at the Albury and District Historical Society and also appears in C. Woods' *Gerogery West to Gerogery*. J. Paxton's *Toorak as I Knew It* and E. M. Robb's *Early Toorak and District* recall life and manners among the grand households of Melbourne's most monied suburb. Chapter 5: An understanding of Chirnside wealth is well obtained through a visit to Werribee Park estate, now open to the public; John Percy Chirnside is an ADB entry 1891–1939. A review of the F. W. Armytage gallery at Wooloomanatta appeared in G. Vaughan's *The Armytage Collection* from Studies in Australian Art, 1978. Chapter 6: National Archives and The Australian War Memorial hold extensive Boer War records, although Bertram Armytage's membership of a British Regiment proved an impediment in tracing his South African service. Correspondence with Lt. Colonel R. J. Binks of The Royal Scots Dragoon Guards, Edinburgh Castle, indicated a gap in record-keeping before 1914. Bertram Armytage's return to Australia is recorded in an army cable message (AWM3 753842) of 18 July 1902, held in National Archives, Canberra. The National Archives at Kew, Surrey, revealed that he received the King's Medal at Bangalore, India on 1 February 1903. M. Barthorp's *The Anglo Boer Wars* is a study of the conflict. S. Limb and P. Cordingley's *Captain Oates, Soldier and Explorer* unfolds a biography of another tragic Antarctic figure who was Boer War warrior and horseman. The Cavalry and Guards Club, London, lists Bertram as a member 1902–1908. Chapter 7: Shackleton's first press interview appeared in Adelaide's *Register* of 7 December 1907. 'Votes and Proceedings of the Commonwealth Parliament', December 1907 cover the grant to the BAE. Herbert Dyce Murphy, an Armytage relative is the subject of two biographies, M. Watson's *The Spy Who Loved Children* and H. Rossiter's *Lady Spy, Gentleman Explorer*. Leila Armytage is discussed in A. Selzer's *The Armytages of Como*.

ANTARCTICA AND THE BAE

Chapters 8–9: During December 1907 news of the BAE appeared almost daily in the *Sydney Morning Herald* and other metropolitan papers. Reports continued from January 1908 until March. Professor David's commissioned articles, delivered by the returning ships appeared as a series in the *Daily Telegraph*. In the Mitchell Library, a letter from Shackleton to C. R. Ford indicates the likelihood of taking Professor David to Antartica (MLMSS6076). S. Neuman's (ed.) *Shackleton's Lieutenant: The Nimrod Diary of A. L. A. Mackintosh* is a valuable contribution to the voyage and reaching McMurdo Sound. The arrangement of the ponies and their equipment are found in seven BAE records of the Polar Collection, South Australian Museum. Chapter 10: The survival of the hut at Cape Royds into the modern era is described in L. B. Quartermain's *The Historic Huts of the Ross Sea*, and booklet and statements issued by Antarctic Heritage Trust of New Zealand, and in D. L. Harrowfield's *Sledging into History*. Marshall's observations of Bertram Armytage are in his BAE diary (MS 1456-8) SPRI. Shackleton summarised the BAE's scientific work in an article for *The Geographical Journal*, London, November 1909. Chapter 11: The making and purpose of the Discovery Hut is described in Scott's *The Voyage of the Discovery* and in D. E. Yelverton's *Antarctica Unveiled*. An amusing article on Professor David's contribution to the BAE appeared in *Polar Record* no. 115 of 1977. On the author's first visit (1958), life had returned to McMurdo Sound through the U.S. Navy's Operation Deep Freeze, the International Geophysical Year and Commonwealth Trans-Antarctic Expedition. The huts of Scott and Shackleton stood much as the explorers had left them nearly 50 years before. Chapter 12: Shackleton's letter is in the Mitchell Library (ML DOC. 1560). Priestly's description of the Western Party and the drifting floe incident are in his BAE diary (298/1/6, 298/1/7, 298/1/8) SPRI. Evans' *Narrative of the Expedition* (SPRI) was written 'at the request of Lady Edgeworth David'. Chapter 13: J. K. Davis in his *High Latitude* describes

events aboard *Nimrod* which led to the finding of the Northern
Party. The BAE's dominant character, after Shackleton, clearly was
Edgeworth David. He contributed the Northern Party narrative to
Shackleton's book. His writings, photographs and scientific papers
are held in University of Sydney Archives, La Trobe Library,
Mitchell Library and Basser Library of the Australian Academy of
Science. Chapter 14: Wild's diary of the Southern Party at SPRI
(944/1), and his memoirs in the Mitchell Library (ML MSS2198/1)
offer a fascinating insight into his BAE experiences. Chapter 15: *The
Australian Philatalist* of 10 July 1909 describes Shackleton's role as
Antarctic postmaster for the New Zealand Government. *Nimrod's*
return to New Zealand began a series of BAE news items in major
newspapers which ran from 24 March until late November.
Professor David who returned to Sydney some three weeks before
Shackleton gave first-hand reports for the Australian press.
Chapter 16: *The Heart of the Antarctic* first appeared in two volumes
in November 1909, followed by a single volume popular edition in
November 1910. B. Riffenburg's *Nimrod* (pp. 282–283) deals with
Shackleton's furthest south sceptics. Shackleton paid for Priestly's
return from London to work with David at the University of Sydney
on writing up the BAE's Vol. 1 geology; raising money to finance
publication was part of the task undertaken for Shackleton. The
Beaullieu Library at the University of Melbourne contains Armytage
family records. The Bertram Armytage will, inquest and probate
documents are held in the Victorian Public Records Office. The
Blanch Armytage letter of 8 May 1910 is held in SPRI.

BIBLIOGRAPHY

Australian Dictionary of Biography, vols 1851–1890; 1891–1939.
Melbourne: Melbourne University Press

Barthorp, M. 1987. *The Anglo-Boer Wars*. London: Blandford Press

Branagan, D. 2005. *T. W. Edgeworth David, A Life*. Canberra: National
Library of Australia

Burke, D. 2005. *Voyage to the End of the World: With Tales from the
Great Ice Barrier*. Boulder, CO: University Press of Colorado

Cannon, M. 1973. *Australia in the Victorian Age: Life in the Country*.
Melbourne: Nelson

Cannon, M. 1975. *Australia in the Victorian Age: Life in the Cities*.
Melbourne: Nelson

Cannon, M. 1985. *The Long Last Summer: Australia's Upper Class
before the Great War*. Melbourne: Nelson

Chapman, Nan. 1965. *Historic Homes of Western Victoria*. Melbourne:
Colac Herald

Cornfield, J. and Collins Persse, M. 1996. *Geelong Grammarians: A
Biographical Register 1855–1913*. Volume 1. Geelong: Geelong
Grammar School

Cox, L. C. 1986. *The Galloping Guns of Rupertswood and Werribee
Park: A History of the Victorian Horse Artillery*. Melbourne: Coonans
Hill Press

David, M. E. 1937. *Professor David: The Life of Sir Edgeworth David.* London: Edward Arnold & Company

David, T. W. E. and Priestly, R. E.. 1914. *British Antarctic Expedition 1907–09. Report of the Scientific Investigations. Geology.* Volume 1. London: William Heinemann

Davis, J. K. 1962. *High Latitude.* Melbourne: Melbourne University Press

de Serville, P. 1991. *Pounds and Pedigrees: Upper Class Victoria 1850–80.* Melbourne: Oxford University Press

Farwell, B. 1976. *The Great Anglo-Boer War.* New York: Harper & Row

Fisher, M and J. 1957 *Shackleton,* London: James Barrie Books

Griffiths, Tom. 2007. *Slicing the Silence.* Sydney: University of NSW Press

Hansard. 1905. Melbourne: Parliament of the Commonwealth

Harrowfield, D. L. 1981. *Sledging into History.* Auckland: MacMillan Co. of New Zealand

Henderson, A. 1936. *Early Pioneer Families of Victoria and Riverina.* Melbourne: McCannon Bird & Co.

Huntford, R. 1985. *Shackleton.* London: Hodder & Staughton

Jacka, F. and E. (ed.). 1988. *Mawson's Antarctic Diaries.* Sydney: Susan Haynes – Allen & Unwin

Joyce, E. M. 1929. *The South Polar Trail.* London: Duckworth & Company

Kiddle, M. 1961. *Men of Yesterday: A Social History of the Western District of Victoria 1834–90.* Melbourne: Melbourne University Press

Limb, S. & Cordingley, P. 1982. *Captain Oates: Soldier and Explorer.* London: B. T. Batesford Ltd

Martin, S. 1996. *A History of Antarctica.* Sydney: State Library Press

Mawer, G. A. 2006. *South by Northwest.* Adelaide: Wakefield Press

Mawson, D. 1915. *The Home of the Blizzard.* 2 vols. London: William Heinemann

McGonigal, D. and Woodworth, L. 2001. *Antarctic, The Complete Story.* Melbourne: Five Mile Press

McNicoll, R. 1988. *Number 36 Collins Street: Melbourne Club 1838–1988*. Sydney: Allen & Unwin

Murray, J. and Marston, G. E. 1913. *Antarctic Days*. London: Andrew Melrose

Neuman, S. (ed.). 1990. *Shackleton's Lieutenant: The Nimrod Diary of A. L. A. Mackintosh*, British Antarctic Expedition 1907–1909. Auckland: Polar Publications

Paxton, J. 1985. *Toorak As I Knew It: 1900–1930*. Melbourne: Prahan Historical and Arts Society

Priestly, R. 1914. *Antarctic Adventure*. London: Allen & Unwin

Quartermain, L. 1963. *Two Huts in the Antarctic*. Wellington: Antarctic Division, NZ Dept Scientific and Industrial Research

Riffenburg, B. 2004. *Nimrod*. London: Bloomsbury

Ronald, H. B. 1978. *Wool Past the Winning Post: The Chirnside Family*. South Yarra: Landvale Enterprises

Ross, J. C. 1847. *A Voyage of Discovery and Research in the Southern and Antarctic Regions*. 2 vols. London: John Murray

Rossiter, H. 2001. *Lady Spy, Gentleman Explorer*. Sydney: Random House

Scott, R. F. 1905. *The Voyage of the Discovery*. 2 vols. London: John Murray

Selzer, A. 2003. *The Armytages of Como*. Melbourne: Halstead Press in association with The National Trust (Vic.)

Serle, G. 1982. *John Monash: A Biography*. Melbourne: Melbourne University Press

Shackleton, E. H. (ed.). 1908. *Aurora Australis*. Cape Royds: BAE

Shackleton, E. H. 1909. *The Heart of the Antarctic*. 2 vols. London: William Heinemann

Watson, M. 1977. *The Spy who loved children: The Enigma of Herbert Dyce Murphy 1879–1971*. Melbourne: Melbourne University Press

Woods, C. (ed.). 1984. *Gerogery West to Gerogery: Centenary of Gerogery Public School*, 1884–1984. Gerogery: Gerogery School Centenary Committee

Wynd, I. 1981. *So Fine a Country: A History of the Shire of Corio*. North Geelong: The Shire of Corio

Yelverton, D. E. 2000. *Antarctica Unveiled: Scott's First Expedition and the Quest for the Unknown Continent*. Boulder, CO: University Press of Colorado

NEWSPAPERS

Age (Melbourne)
Argus (Melbourne)
Daily Telegraph (Sydney)
Geelong Advertiser
Register (Adelaide)
Sydney Morning Herald
The Times (London)

RECORDS

Australian Antarctic Division (Hobart)
Latrobe Library (Melbourne)
Melbourne Church of England Grammar School (*Liber Melburnensis*)
Melbourne University Archives, document and pictorial
Mitchell Library (Sydney)
Museum Victoria (Melbourne)
National Archives of Australia (Canberra, Melbourne)
National Trust of Australia (Vic.), Como, South Yarra
Royal Historical Society of Victoria (Melbourne)
Scott Polar Research Institute (University of Cambridge)
South Australian Museum, Adelaide (Mawson papers)
Turnbull Library (Wellington)

PERIODICALS

'Antarctic' (New Zealand Antarctic Society)
'The Australian Philatelist' (1908–1909)
'The Home' (1931)
'The Polar Record'
'Table Talk' (Melbourne, 1888, 1895)

GLOSSARY OF POLAR TERMS

BAE: British Antarctic Expedition.

blue ice: hard glacier ice, bluish in tone and exceedingly slippery to walk on when free of snow.

crevasse: a deep split in the surface of an ice sheet or glacier, often hidden beneath a snow bridge.

drift: wind-blown snow.

feldspar: various rock-forming minerals occurring in igneous, sedimentary and metamorphic rocks; these may consist of silicates of aluminium, with potassium, sodium and calcium.

finnesko: reindeer-skin boots worn with fur on the outside, introduced originally by Laplanders for traversing soft snow; sennegrass cushioned the interiors.

heliograph: a mirror device for sending morse-code messages by reflecting the sunlight.

hoosh: a soup-like mixture consisting of pemmican mixed with water and the addition of oatmeal, bacon and cheese and other ingredients, depending on the rations on the sledge.

hummocked ice: pressure-driven ice pack erupting in broken, irregular mounds.

ice: ice foot – old ice attached to the coast; fast ice – extension of sea ice beyond ice foot; sea ice – frozen sea, later broken into separate drifting pack ice; floes – floating platforms of pack ice.

Maujee ration: an extra feed for BAE's ponies, consisting of dried beef, currants, carrots, milk and sugar.

man-hauling: towing a sledge with harness and ropes using human power.

moraine: glacier-borne boulders and stones dumped in a particular location.

Nansen cooker: devised by the Norwegian explorer, consists of an aluminium chamber holding a smaller chamber within.

nunatak: a major rock outcrop rising through the icesheet, normally part of a sub-ice mountainous section.

pemmican: a compressed cake of dried meat and fat or lard carried on sledging trips, as an ingredient for making hoosh.

plasmon: a trade-name biscuit with a soluble milk protein ingredient to supplement sledging rations.

Plimsoll line: a line drawn on a ship's hull indicating the legal limit to which it may be safely loaded.

pressure ridge: blocks of ice forced upwards in collision between fast ice and sea ice.

rotifer: minute, multi-cellular aquatic organisms.

sastrugi: hard ridges of wind-blown snow, varying in depth according to weather and exposed surface.

skua gull: a large predatory bird found in coastal areas that attacks penguin eggs or young.

snow bridge: an unstable platform or arch-like covering above a crevasse.

trace: the connection of rope or strap between the sledge and dog or man-hauling team.

INDEX

BLOOD BROTHERS

THE ANZAC GENESIS

Jeff Hopkins-Weise

By the middle of the nineteenth century, the very existence of European colonial settlement in New Zealand was under threat.

With Queen Victoria's British forces stretched thinly across the globe, the New Zealand colony had to look to its sister colonial states in Australia for support.

This ground-breaking work shows, for the first time in detail, how the military, social and economic brotherhood later embodied in the notion of the Anzac spirit began not on the sandy beaches of Gallipoli but 50 years earlier in the damp forests and fields of the North Island of New Zealand.

ISBN 978 1 86254 838 1

For more information visit www.wakefieldpress.com.au

SOUTH BY NORTHWEST

THE MAGNETIC CRUSADE AND THE CONTEST FOR ANTARCTICA

Granville Allen Mawer

For many, Antarctic history begins and ends with the race between Scott and Amundsen for the geographic south pole, but they were late to the start and only briefly on the course. By then, another polar race had already been in progress for seventy years, and it would continue for even longer. That race, for the South Magnetic Pole, was a marathon rather than a sprint and its starting point was suitably distant from Antarctica, in the ice of the fabled Northwest Passage.

South by Northwest tells the riveting story of the competition between rival nations – the British, French and Americans – to claim Antarctica's holy grail. In this never-before-told tale of ambition and achievement, maritime historian Allen Mawer resolves some of the controversies that have festered for the past 160 years.

ISBN 978 1 86254 650 9

For more information visit www.wakefieldpress.com.au

ONE COMMON ENEMY

The *Laconia* Incident: A Survivor's Memoir

Jim McLoughlin with David Gibb

'I'll see the world,' Jim McLoughlin told his parents as he set off to join the Royal Navy in 1939. 'It'll be fun.'

Months later, this Liverpool lad was sailing to war aboard the massive battleship HMS *Valiant*. He saw some of the world, but it wasn't fun.

In *One Common Enemy*, he recounts how the chaos and carnage of war at sea in the Norwegian and Mediterranean campaigns led him to a fateful rendezvous with a much-loved ship from his boyhood, the passenger liner *Laconia*. Nostalgia turned to disaster when Laconia was torpedoed by a German U-boat in the South Atlantic. Despite a remarkable rescue attempt by a courageous, compassionate foe, Jim was condemned to a drifting lifeboat and a harrowing voyage of death and madness.

One Common Enemy is a story of a desperate personal battle for survival, but also a moving narrative of innocence lost and a lifelong battle with confronting memories.

ISBN 978 1 86254 690 5

For more information visit www.wakefieldpress.com.au

SHACKLETON'S BOAT JOURNEY

F. A. Worsley

This is the classic account of Sir Ernest Shackleton's ill-fated Antarctic expedition of 1914–16 told by Frank Worsley, captain of the expedition ship, *Endurance*.

First trapped then crushed by ice, the *Endurance* drifted in an ice floe for five months before reaching the barren and inhospitable Elephant Island. Certain that no rescue party would ever find them, Shackleton, Worsely and four others set off in a small boat for South Georgia, the nearest inhabited island, leaving behind 22 men whose survival depended on the success of this desperate gamble.

In a remarkable feat of courage and fortitude, they made the 800-mile journey in just two weeks under the most appalling conditions imaginable, including hurricane-force winds, fifty-foot waves and sub-zero temperatures. *Shackleton's Boat Journey* vividly recreates this extraordinary story of survival and paints a vivid portrait of one of the world's greatest explorers.

ISBN 978 1 86254 775 9

For more information visit www.wakefieldpress.com.au

Wakefield Press is an independent publishing and
distribution company based in Adelaide, South Australia.
We love good stories and publish beautiful books.
To see our full range of titles, please visit our website at
www.wakefieldpress.com.au.